Trash TO TREASURE

*E*nliven your home and garden with unique accessories and novelties. It's easy — and inexpensive — with the creative ideas in this book and a little "trash." Friends will "ooh" and "aah" over your lovely lamps, whimsical plant pokes, stylish vases, attractive organizers, and more. But they'll be even more impressed to learn that you made it all using recycled materials! This inventive volume of Trash to Treasure presents easy-to-understand instructions and full-color photography to guide you from start to finish. Five fabulous sections contain loads of crafty creations. All Through the House will dress up your home with clever notions for every nook and cranny, while Soft and Simple is full of fantastic ideas involving fabric scraps and old linens. Turn to Creative Touches for imaginative items like jewelry and garden décor. You'll find striking furniture makeovers in Second Chances, and Celebrations offers splendid ideas for special occasions. With dozens of inspiring projects to choose from, you'll be creating "recycled" treasures in no time. So turn the page and let the fun begin!

LEISURE ARTS, INC.
Little Rock, Arkansas

EDITORIAL STAFF

Vice President and Editor-in-Chief: Sandra Graham Case
Executive Director of Publications: Cheryl Nodine Gunnells
Director of Designer Relations: Debra Nettles
Design Director: Cyndi Hansen
Editorial Director: Susan Frantz Wiles
Publications Director: Kristine Anderson Mertes
Photography Director: Lori Ringwood Dimond
Art Operations Director: Jeff Curtis
Director of Public Relations & Retail Marketing: Stephen Wilson

DESIGN
Design Manager: Diana Sanders Cates
Design Captains: Cherece Athy, Polly Tullis Browning, and Peggy Elliott Cunningham
Designers: Anne Pulliam Stocks, Linda Diehl Tiano, Claudia I. Wendt, and Becky Werle
Design Assistant: Lucy Combs Beaudry
Production Assistant: Karla Edgar

TECHNICAL
Managing Editor: Leslie Schick Gorrell
Book Coordinator and Senior Technical Writer: Shawnna B. Manes

Technical Writers: Stacey Robertson Marshall, Jennifer Potts Hutchings, Christina Price Kirkendoll, Jean W. Lewis, Linda Luder, and Theresa Hicks Young
Technical Associates: Andrea Ahlen and Kimberly J. Smith

EDITORIAL
Managing Editor: Alan Caudle
Associate Editor: Kimberly L. Ross

ART
Art Publications Director: Rhonda Shelby
Art Imaging Director: Mark Hawkins
Art Category Manager: Lora Puls
Lead Graphic Artist: Elaine Barry Wheat
Imaging Technicians: Stephanie Johnson and Mark Potter
Staff Photographer: Russell Ganser
Photography Stylists: Janna Laughlin and Cassie Newsome
Publishing Systems Administrator: Becky Riddle
Publishing Systems Assistants: Clint Hanson, Myra Means, and Chris Wertenberger

BUSINESS STAFF

Publisher: Rick Barton
Vice President, Finance: Tom Siebenmorgen
Director of Corporate Planning and Development: Laticia Mull Cornett
Vice President, Retail Marketing: Bob Humphrey
Vice President, Sales: Ray Shelgosh
Vice President, National Accounts: Pam Stebbins

Director of Sales and Services: Margaret Reinold
Vice President, Operations: Jim Dittrich
Comptroller, Operations: Rob Thieme
Retail Customer Service Managers: Sharon Hall and Stan Raynor
Print Production Manager: Fred F. Pruss

Library of Congress Catalog Number 98-65089
International Standard Book Number 1-57486-277-4

10 9 8 7 6 5 4 3 2 1

all through the house 6

PATRIOTIC PAPER ART 8
Patriotic Paper Collage
COFFEE CAN LAMPSHADE......................10
Coffee Can Lampshade
CUT-OUT CANDLE LAMP 11
Can Luminary with Jar Votive
PARADISE PENCIL HOLDER......................12
Soda-Can Palm Tree and Pencil Hut
MATCHBOX MINI CHEST............................14
Matchbox Desk Organizer
PRETTY POSTAL CENTER..........................16
Mailing Center
JAZZY JEAN LETTERS 18
Denim-Covered Wall Letters
MOTTLED BOTTLE VASES 19
Painted Bottle Vases
WRISTWATCH WALL CLOCK 20
Wristwatch Wall Clock

CHEERFUL SHEERS...................................22
Curtains
Framed Print
SCRAPBOOKING BOXES............................24
Covered Boxes
ELEGANT ACCENT TABLE 26
Coffee Can Table and Soda-Can Vine
PHOTOGRAPHER'S MYSTERY COLLAGE 28
Brown Paper Frame
EYE-CATCHING OUTDOOR CHARM 29
Outdoor Jewelry Decoration
FISHIN' FOR PHOTOS................................30
Cardbord Fishing Pole
Recycled Frames
Cardboard Stands for Frames
Soda-Can Trout
Stringer of Fish

soft and simple 34

SOOTHING EYE BUTTERFLY......................36
Tablecloth Eye Soother
KEEN JEAN BOLSTER................................38
Denim Bolster Pillow
LOVABLE LAMB 39
Chenille and Sock Scraps Lamb
BLOOMING COMFORTS 40
Tablecloth Pillows
VINTAGE VOGUE SHIRT 42
Vintage Fabric-Embellished Shirt
TEA TIME VEST 44
Appliquéd Coverlet Vest
PRIORITY PAPERWEIGHTS 45
Leather Paperweights
"SEW-SENSATIONAL" ORGANIZER 46
Placemat Needlework Organizer

HANDY BAG HANGER...............................48
Hanging Storage Bag
"CAN-DO" PIN CUSHION..........................49
Pin Cushion-Topped Can Notions Holder
RUGGED RAG RUGS................................50
Scrap Oval Rug
Planned Oval Rug

creative touches 52

FLOATING FLOWER CANDLES 54
   Floating Flower Candles

PERKY PLANT POKES.............................55
   Aluminum Can Flower Plant Pokes

GLORIOUS GARDEN ANGELS.....................56
   Aluminum Angel Plant Pokes

TIMELY MOSAIC 58
   Mosaic-Tiled Saucer Clock

HEARTFELT KEEPSAKE BOX 59
   Studded Cigar Box

EMBOSSED HEARTS JEWELRY 60
   Aluminum Can Jewelry

HEAVENLY HIDEAWAY PENDANT 62
   Matchbox Pendant

HANDSOME HINGED BOX........................63
   Egg-Carton Trinket Keeper

ATTRACTIVE ORGANIZER 64
   Cardboard Bill Organizer

EXOTIC ELEPHANT VASE 66
   Shredded Paper Vase

YEAR BOOK FRAME...............................68
   Book Cover Frame

DENIM DESK ORGANIZERS 69
   Denim-Covered Containers

REMINDER MAGNETS.............................70
   Plastic Message Boards and Marker Holder

EASY ABSTRACT ART 71
   Framed Quilt-Block Paper Art

BIRD BUNGALOWS................................72
   Plastic Bottle Birdhouses

LUMINOUS LANTERN 74
   Coffee Can Luminary

ETHEREAL ANGEL.................................76
   Paper Shelf Sitter

NOSTALGIC NOTIONS COLLECTION 77
   Craft Scraps Collage

FUNNY FACE MOBILE.............................78
   Plastic Lid Faces Mobile

second chances 80

"DRESS UP" LEARNING CENTER 82
   Ottoman Learning Center

HINGED TOWEL BAR 84
   Table Leg Towel Holder

SPLISH-SPLASH STOOL............................85
   Painted Stool

BREAKFAST-IN-BED TRAY 86
   Framed Bed Tray

CACTUS FLOWER PICNIC CADDY 88
   Cap-Studded Serving Crate

FLASHY PHOTO FRAMES 89
   Can Embellished Frames

FAUX-FINISH FLOOR LAMP 90
   Faux-Finished Brass Floor Lamp
   and Lampshade Cover

NIFTY BELTED NAPKINS 92
   Belt Napkin Rings with Napkins

TEXTURED SPHERES 93
   Textured Plastic Balls

PLAYFUL PILLARS 94
   Game Piece-Covered Candles

"NOTE-WORTHY" MOSAIC TABLE 95
   Button Mosaic Table

celebrations 96

"BE MINE" VALENTINE BOX......................98
Candy Box Valentine Container
SENTIMENTAL HEARTS...........................100
Aluminum Can Pins
"EGGS-TRAORDINARY" EASTER BASKET..101
Découpaged Plastic Basket
ENCHANTING SPRING TREE....................102
Aluminum Can Tree
ALL-AMERICAN ART..............................104
Painted Vinyl Wall Hanging
ALL-STAR LIBERTY WREATH....................105
Plastic Foam Wreath
"EERIE-SISTIBLE" HALLOWEEN LAMP.....106
Halloween Jar Lamp
"SPOOK-TACULAR" SPIDER....................108
Plastic Spider
LI'L BUTTERFLY COSTUME.....................110
Tablecloth Butterfly Costume
STYLISH GIFT DRESSINGS.....................112
Marbleized Paper for Gift Wrap and Tags
PLACE CARD PARTY FAVORS...................113
Paper-Covered Boxes
ITTY-BITTY GIFT BOXES........................114
Recycled Cards Gift Boxes
CREATIVE GIFT TOTE............................115
Cut-Out Gift Box
ROYAL FORTRESS.................................116
Cardboard Castle Centerpiece
PARTY DOLL.......................................118
Bottle Cap Doll
STARRY TOPIARY.................................119
Natural Topiary Tree
FROSTY FLEECE PALS...........................120
Fleece-Covered Can Snowmen
SHIMMERING CD ORNAMENT.................122
CD Christmas Ornament

ORNAMENTAL BLOCK............................123
Milk Carton Ornament
ANGELIC SNOWMAN TREE TOPPER.........124
Lid Snowman Tree Topper
JOLLY SNOWMAN CANDLEHOLDER..........125
Drinking Glass Candleholder Jar
ENLIGHTENING ORNAMENTS..................126
Lightbulb Ornaments

PATTERNS...128
GENERAL INSTRUCTIONS........................151
INDEX...158
CREDITS..160

all
through
the
house

From bedroom to bath and dining room to den, a little "trash" can add a distinctive touch to any room. Torn pieces of magazine pages form memorable art, crimped aluminum cans find a practical new function, and a little ingenuity turns assorted items into fanciful home accessories. The creative accents in this section will add a whole new dimension to your décor.

PATRIOTIC PAPER ART

Pledge your allegiance to the land that you love with a stirring collage. Fashion a landscape with bits of paper torn from out-of-date magazines or advertising circulars, then add a sprinkling of words that express what America means to you. Enhance with a store-bought mat and frame, and your patriotic heart art is ready to display.

PATRIOTIC PAPER COLLAGE

Recycled items: assorted magazines, wooden picture frame to fit an 11" x 14" picture, and an 11" x 14" piece of cardboard for frame backing

You will also need an 8½" x 11" piece of card stock, plastic zipper bags, paintbrushes, craft glue, tweezers, tracing paper, stylus, transfer paper, coordinating double mat to fit an 8" x 10" picture, gold paint pen, green and ivory acrylic paint, and tape.

Refer to Painting Techniques, page 151, before beginning project. Allow glue and paint to dry after each application.

1. For design, enlarge pattern, page 128, by 154%, and photocopy onto card stock.

2. Using suggested colors in Color Key, remove pages from magazines and sort according to color. Tear colored areas of pages into ¼" pieces (we put each color into a plastic bag).

3. Working in small sections, use a paintbrush to apply glue to pattern. Use tweezers to place paper pieces on glue, overlapping slightly. For shaded areas, glue torn word pieces to design according to pattern. Repeat until design is covered.

4. Tear patriotic words and stars from magazines and glue them in place.

5. Trace words pattern, page 128, onto tracing paper. Use stylus and transfer paper to transfer words along bottom of mat; draw over words with paint pen.

6. Paint frame green; *Dry Brush* frame using a mixture of two parts ivory paint and one part green paint.

7. Tape collage in opening of mat and insert mat into frame; secure backing in frame.

COLOR KEY

white	light green	light blue with words
white with words	medium green	medium blue
light yellow	dark green	dark blue
light yellow with words	yellow green	red
dark yellow	green with colors	light lavender
dark yellow with words	pale blue	pink lavender
pale green	light blue	lavender

COFFEE CAN LAMPSHADE

*B*ona fide coffee-holics will love *our refreshing "light" brew! Simply made from a rust-colored coffee can, this tasteful lampshade offers a "latte" style in a little space. The final touch: safety pin and sparkly bead trim.*

COFFEE CAN LAMPSHADE

Recycled items: a natural sponge, large coffee can with both ends removed, toothbrush, $3/4$"-long gold safety pins, beaded trim pieces; and small gauge wire scraps

You will also need rust-colored spray primer; orange, dark orange, and bronze acrylic paint; matte clear acrylic spray sealer; clip lamp hardware; needle-nose pliers; assorted glass beads; seed beads; wire cutters; 20-gauge craft wire; and a hammer and awl.

Refer to Painting Techniques, page 151, before beginning project. Allow paint to dry after each application.

1. For lampshade, follow *Rusting* to paint can; *Spatter Paint* can bronze.

2. Insert lamp hardware inside lampshade.

3. For beaded dangles, use needle-nose pliers to straighten safety pins and crimp clasp of each pin.

4. For each dangle, thread one glass bead on safety pin, then thread rest of pin with assorted seed beads, leaving $3/8$" of pin unbeaded. Using wire cutters, clip point of pin, then use pliers to form a loop.

5. For beaded trim, measure circumference of can and add 3". Cut a piece of 20-gauge craft wire the determined measurement.

6. Remove beads from trim pieces. Plan a beading pattern for beaded trim according to available beads (ours has approximately $5/8$" of beads between dangles).

7. Loop one end of wire piece to prevent beads from slipping off; thread beads and dangles onto wire.

8. To hang beaded trim from shade, punch a small hole in front and back of bottom edge of can. Wrap trim around bottom edge of can; using needle-nose pliers, twist ends tightly together. Thread wire scraps around beaded trim and through each hole; twist wire ends inside can to secure.

CUT-OUT CANDLE LAMP

With a craft knife and a little paint, a large aluminum can is transformed into this decorative votive holder! A small glass jar cradles your candle, while floral cut-outs, reminiscent of folk art, create flickering light patterns. Amber beads add elegance.

CAN LUMINARY WITH JAR VOTIVE

Recycled items: a 25.4-oz. aluminum beverage can, natural sponge, and a glass jar to fit inside luminary

You will also need utility scissors, craft knife and cutting mat, tape, fine-point permanent pen, awl, rust-colored spray primer, orange and dark orange acrylic paint, matte clear acrylic spray sealer, needle-nose pliers, wire cutters, 24-gauge copper wire, 34-gauge gold craft wire, seed beads, and larger translucent beads.

Refer to Painting Techniques, page 151, before beginning project.

1. Cutting through opening in can, cut down side of can to bottom rim. Cut away and discard top and bottom of can; flatten remaining piece.

2. Trace flower pattern, page 129, onto tracing paper. Using craft knife, cut out grey areas as indicated on pattern. Tape pattern to printed side of can piece; using pen, draw around pattern onto can piece. Remove pattern from can piece.

3. Using craft knife, score can piece along pattern lines, then turn it over and finish cutting through can along scored lines. Using awl, punch holes in can piece where indicated on pattern.

4. Follow *Rusting* to paint can piece.

5. Tie ends of can piece together with copper wire, twisting wire ends to secure.

6. For each dangle, cut a 2" length of gold wire. Thread wire through seed bead; bring both ends of wire up through larger bead. Thread one end of wire from outside to inside through hole in luminary and twist ends of wire together on inside to secure.

7. Place jar in luminary.

PARADISE PENCIL HOLDER

*L*et your thoughts occasionally drift off to an island paradise with this breezy desk organizer. An aluminum-can palm tree provides a bit of shade, while a coffee-can "hut" holds a wealth of pencils, pens, and other desk necessities. Tiny shells and starfish are seaworthy embellishments. "Beachy-keen"!

SODA-CAN PALM TREE AND PENCIL HUT

Recycled items: fourteen aluminum beverage cans; $13^1/2$" x $^3/4$" dia. dowel or wood piece for trunk; 13-oz. coffee can; corrugated cardboard; starfish, shells, or other embellishments

You will also need utility scissors; drill and bits; oval wooden plaque (ours measures $8^3/4$" x $5^1/2$"); craft crimper (for paper and lightweight metal); decorative-edge craft scissors; needle-nose pliers; rust-colored spray primer for metal; grey and green spray paint; paintbrushes; light green, yellow, light brown, and red acrylic paint; matte clear acrylic spray sealer; #4 carpet tacks; tracing paper; craft foam; stylus; pushpin; 18-gauge floral wire; and wood glue.

Refer to Painting Techniques, page 151, before beginning project. Allow primer, paint, sealer, and glue to dry after each application.

1. Cutting through openings in cans, cut down side of each can to bottom rim. Cut away and discard tops and bottoms of cans; flatten remaining pieces.

2. For trunk, drill $1^1/2$" deep hole in top center of dowel. Attach trunk to plaque.

3. For tree bark, cut seventeen $1^1/4$"w strips the length of can pieces; crimp strips. Using craft scissors, trim one long edge of each strip (bottom edge). Using pliers, pinch every fourth and fifth ridge together along top edge to curve strip. Set three strips aside for hut roof.

4. Apply primer to bark strips; paint grey, then *Dry Brush* light green. Apply sealer to strips.

5. Starting at base of trunk, wrap first strip around trunk; overlap end of strip at back of trunk and secure with a tack. Overlapping edges enough to cover tacks, continue attaching strips to trunk until covered.

6. For leaves, trace pattern, page 130, onto tracing paper; cut out. Using pattern, cut eight leaves from can pieces.

7. To emboss each leaf, place leaf on craft foam. Place pattern on leaf, then use stylus to draw over lines of pattern and use pushpin to punch hole in leaf where indicated. Use utility scissors to cut small notches in edges of leaves.

8. For each leaf, make a small loop at one end of a 9" length of wire. Inserting straight end of wire through hole, glue wire along back side of leaf.

9. Apply primer to leaves; paint back sides light green. Paint tops green, then accent edges with yellow. Apply sealer to leaves.

10. Fill hole in trunk with glue, then insert wire ends of leaves into hole; shape leaves.

11. For pencil holder, apply primer to inside of coffee can. Cut a 5" x $13^1/2$" piece of cardboard. Remove one side of cardboard, exposing corrugations; apply primer, then *Dry Brush* ridges light brown. Glue cardboard around can.

12. Apply primer to three roof strips, then *Dry Brush* red. Glue top edge along top of can. Apply sealer to pencil holder.

13. Glue pencil holder and embellishments on plaque.

MATCHBOX MINI CHEST

*T*here's a place for everything when you're using our dandy desktop organizer. Heavy-duty cardboard holds pencils or pens, and eight large matchboxes become drawers for rubber bands, paper clips, and all your other desk supplies. A little paint and some salvaged wrapping paper enhance this mini chest's aesthetic appeal.

MATCHBOX DESK ORGANIZER

Recycled items: eight large matchboxes, gift wrap, heavy-duty cardboard, wallpaper scraps, eight paper clips, and four same-size plastic beverage bottle caps

You will also need spray primer, craft glue stick, hot glue gun, paintbrush, acrylic paint, and a pushpin.

Use hot glue for all gluing unless otherwise indicated. Allow primer, glue stick, and paint to dry after each application.

1. Remove drawers from matchbox covers; set aside.

2. Apply primer to each matchbox cover. Using glue stick, cover boxes with gift wrap, folding and gluing excess paper inside box.

3. Cut two 7³/₄" squares from cardboard; cover completely with wallpaper.

4. For bottom layer, refer to Fig. 1 to glue four matchbox covers to one piece of cardboard.

Fig. 1

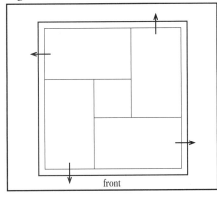

front

5. For top layer, refer to Fig. 2 to glue remaining matchbox covers to second piece of cardboard.

Fig. 2

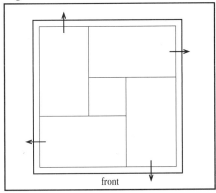

front

6. Glue top layer to bottom layer.

7. Paint drawers. Using pushpin, make hole in center of each drawer front. For drawer handles, straighten paper clips, then wrap around a pencil to curl. Compress curled paper clips and insert into holes; secure on inside of drawers with glue. Insert drawers into matchbox covers.

8. For pencil holder, cut a 4¹/₄" x 9¹/₂" piece from cardboard. Paint one side; cover remaining side with gift wrap. Referring to Fig. 3, fold cardboard (gift wrap facing out) to fit in hole between matchboxes; glue along flap to hold shape. Glue holder into hole at center of organizer.

Fig. 3

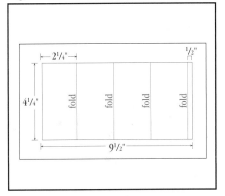

9. For feet, paint bottle caps. Glue caps to bottom corners of organizer.

PRETTY POSTAL CENTER

Our mini mailing center keeps your letter-writing supplies within reach. A favorite pen, stored in a cardboard pants-hanger tube, is always at your fingertips. Seal envelopes with a moistened sponge, stowed away in a plastic bottle cap. A tiny mailbox, complete with foam-scrap flag, holds a roll of stamps. "Write" on!

MAILING CENTER

Recycled items: cardboard tubing from pants hanger, cardboard ring box with lid, $1^3/_4$" dia. plastic bottle cap, solid color fabric scrap, and a white craft foam scrap

You will also need a miter box and craft saw, $1^1/_2$"h and $1^3/_8$"h wooden spools, sandpaper, tack cloth, primer, paintbrushes, acrylic paints to coordinate with fabric, $2^1/_2$" x 10" wooden plaque, wood glue, black permanent fine-point pen, spray adhesive, craft knife and cutting mat, and a compressed craft sponge.

Use wood glue for all gluing unless otherwise indicated. Allow primer, paint, and glue to dry after each application.

1. Using miter box, cut two 2" pieces from cardboard tubing; cut one end of one section at a 45-degree angle. Cut one end from $1^1/_2$" spool. Lightly sand spool; wipe with tack cloth.

2. For penholder, glue cut spool end to one end of plaque. Glue angled end of tube piece to top of spool end.

3. For stamp holder base, glue $1^3/_8$" spool to center of plaque. Glue remaining tube piece to top of spool.

4. For stamp holder top, cut a hole in bottom of ring box slightly smaller than end of tube on base. Using spray adhesive, follow Steps 1 – 7 of Covered Boxes, page 25, to cover ring box and lid with fabric. Cut an X through fabric covering hole in bottom of box; glue end of tube into hole in box. With lid on box, cut an opening in front of box for stamps to slide through.

5. For sponge, draw around cap on sponge; cut out circle just inside drawn line. Glue cap to end of plaque.

6. Apply primer to mailing center, then paint pieces desired base colors.

7. Paint vines with leaves on stamp holder base; use black pen to add details. Paint a door and flowers on box. Cut flag from foam and paint a flower on flag; glue flag to side of box lid.

8. Paint flowers on penholder base, then paint stripes on sponge holder. Wet sponge and place in cap.

JAZZY JEAN LETTERS

Groovy denim letters are perfect for personalizing a pre-teen's room! Fashion letters from layered cardboard, using your favorite computer font as a pattern. Cover with denim or fabric scraps and decorate any way you like. What a fun way to play the "name game"!

DENIM-COVERED WALL LETTERS

Recycled items: corrugated cardboard, denim clothing, and craft foam scraps

You will also need craft glue, tracing paper, pom-poms, chenille stems, and decorative appliqués and accents.

Allow glue to dry after each application.

1. For letter patterns, enlarge computer or printed font to desired size; print letters and cut out (our K measures 12$\frac{1}{2}$" tall).

2. For each letter, draw around pattern three times on cardboard; cut out, then stack and glue cardboard letters together.

3. Cut off any double seams close to seam and remove pockets; set seams and pockets aside.

4. Clipping curves and gluing edges to back, cover one end of letter with denim piece.

5. For next denim piece, glue one edge $\frac{1}{4}$" to wrong side. Overlapping raw edge, repeat Step 4 to glue piece to letter. Continue covering with strips until letter is covered.

6. Add a pocket to one or more letters. Piecing as necessary, glue seam pieces along sides of letters.

7. For each flower, trace pattern, page 131, onto tracing paper; cut out. Draw around pattern onto foam; cut out. Glue pom-pom to flower for center and chenille stem to flower for stem. Place flower in pocket.

8. Glue assorted appliqués and accents on letters as desired.

MOTTLED BOTTLE VASES

*F*resh posies look perfectly sweet in our vibrant bottle vases. Just paint an empty jar in cheerful candy colors, then hide the threaded edge with a ring of ribbon. This winsome accent promises to enliven the patio, guestroom, or any nook or cranny.

PAINTED BOTTLE VASES

Recycled items: assorted bottles, natural sponge, and a toothbrush

You will also need rubbing alcohol, white spray primer, assorted colors of acrylic paint, hot glue gun, matte clear acrylic spray sealer, and ribbon.

Refer to Painting Techniques, page 151, before beginning project. Allow paint and sealer to dry after each application.

1. Clean bottles with alcohol, then apply primer to bottles.

2. *Sponge Paint* each bottle with two coats of paint, then *Spatter Paint* each bottle with a coordinating color.

3. Apply sealer to bottles.

4. Glue end of a length of ribbon to threaded edge of bottle and wrap around bottle three times; fold end at back and glue to secure.

WRISTWATCH WALL CLOCK

This working timepiece will have everyone "watching" the clock. Fashion a first-rate wristband from foam, foam core, and denim. For the quick-to-fix face, fit a purchased clock kit in a painted cookie tin and embellish with a plastic bottle cap stem. The grand finale: old watchcases mark the quarter-hours!

WRISTWATCH WALL CLOCK

Recycled items: a 2¹/₂"h x 7¹/₄" dia. cookie tin (we used a gold tin), four men's wristwatches with bands removed, plastic soda bottle cap, two pants hangers with cardboard tubes, two 13" x 26" pieces of denim (we used pants legs), and black felt scraps

You will also need white spray primer, paintbrushes, ivory metal paint, drill and bits, clock movements kit and hands large enough to fit clock face, craft glue for metal and paint, gold spray paint, foam core, heavy-duty wire cutters, 1"-thick foam, fabric glue, tracing paper, and black acrylic paint.

Use fabric glue for all gluing unless otherwise indicated. Allow primer, craft glue, and paint to dry after each application.

1. Remove lid from tin. Apply primer to outside bottom of tin; paint ivory. Drill a hole through center of tin and, referring to Fig. 1, drill holes for wristband attachments on opposite sides of tin.

Fig. 1

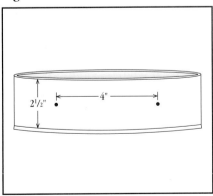

2. Follow manufacturer's instructions to attach clock module and hands to tin. Set watches to three, six, nine, and twelve o'clock. Use craft glue to adhere watches to tin accordingly.

3. For stem, paint bottle cap gold. Draw around cap on foam core; cut out circle just inside drawn line. Using craft glue, glue circle just inside cap; glue cap to side of tin at three o'clock position.

4. For each watchband attachment, remove cardboard tube from hanger. Referring to Fig. 2, cut a 5" section from tube, then cut ends from hanger. Re-insert wire pieces into 5" tube. Working from outside to inside of tin, refer to Fig. 3 to insert wire ends through tin; bend to secure. Place lid on tin.

Fig. 2

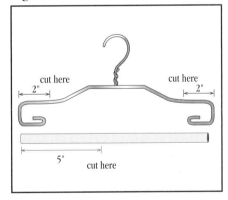

Fig. 3

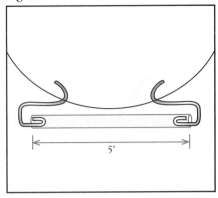

5. For each watchband, cut a 5" x 18" piece of foam, tapering one end to 3" wide. Leaving 4" of fabric at each end, center and glue denim piece around foam. Fold excess denim at wider end over cardboard tube and glue to back of watchband.

6. For bottom band, glue excess denim at narrow end to back of band; glue three felt circles to band.

7. For top band, cut a 2¹/₂" x 11¹/₂" strip of denim for keeper loop; overlaping slightly, glue long edges together. Wrap strip around band and glue at back.

8. For buckle, trace patterns, page 131, onto tracing paper; cut out. Draw around patterns onto foam core; cut out. Paint buckle pieces black.

9. Fold excess denim at top over straight side of buckle and glue to back of band. Center and use craft glue to glue buckle stem to buckle.

CHEERFUL SHEERS

*S*tamp out ho-hum décor! Carefree flowers brighten a wall with their captivating beauty and breathe new life into plain purchased sheers. Construct your own floral stamps from foam packing material and corrugated cardboard. Packing-peanut halves are perfect for stamping lovely leaves.

STAMPED FLORALS

CURTAINS

Recycled items: five 64-oz. plastic juice bottles (bottom of each bottle should resemble a flower), two paper egg cartons, poster board scraps, corrugated cardboard scraps, foam packing material, and a figure eight-shaped foam packing peanut, cut in half

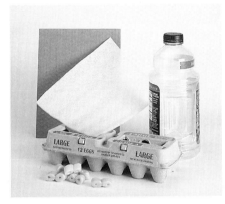

You will also need utility scissors, two buckets, rubber gloves, blender, white spray primer, fine-grit sandpaper, tack cloth, paintbrushes, assorted colors of fabric paint, hot glue gun, jewelry pin backs, tab-top curtain, and tracing paper.

1. For curtain toppers, cut bottoms from bottles 1" from bottom to make flower molds.

2. Tear egg cartons into ¹/₂" pieces; place in bucket. Fill bucket with hot water and allow to soak for at least one hour.

3. Wearing rubber gloves, squeeze excess water from a small handful of pre-soaked paper pieces and place in blender; cover with water until blender is half full. Blend at low speed for fifteen seconds, increasing speed to medium, then high, at fifteen-second intervals; decrease speed in the same manner. When pulp is no longer lumpy, pour into second bucket. Repeat blending process until all pieces have been processed.

4. Scoop pulp from second bucket, then squeeze excess water from mixture. Fill flower molds to slightly heaping and allow to dry.

5. Remove curtain toppers carefully from molds; apply primer, then lightly sand and wipe with tack cloth.

6. Paint toppers desired color, then paint flower petals and centers desired colors. Draw around toppers onto poster board; cut out circles just inside drawn lines. Glue circles to backs of toppers; glue pin backs to center of circles.

7. Paint stems at base of curtain.

8. For flower stamp, trace pattern, page 131, onto tracing paper; cut out. Draw around pattern onto foam; cut out. Cut two circles from cardboard the same size as foam piece. Glue cardboard circles together; glue foam piece to cardboard circles.

9. Using paintbrush, apply paint to stamp; stamp flowers onto curtain on and around stems. Using edge of packing peanut, stamp leaves along stems.

FRAMED PRINT

Recycled items: foam packing material, corrugated cardboard scraps, and a figure eight-shaped foam packing peanut, cut in half

You will also need tracing paper, hot glue gun, pre-cut mat to fit in frame, watercolor paper, paintbrushes, assorted colors of fabric paint, kneaded eraser, and a frame with glass and backing.

1. For flower stamp, trace pattern, page 131, onto tracing paper; cut out. Draw around pattern onto foam; cut out. Cut two circles from cardboard the same size as foam piece. Glue cardboard circles together; glue foam piece to cardboard circles.

2. Lightly draw around openings in mat onto watercolor paper. Using paintbrush, apply paint to stamp; stamp flower onto watercolor paper within marked areas. Paint stem below flower; using edge of packing peanut, stamp leaves along stem. Erase drawn lines from watercolor paper.

3. Center and secure print in mat, then insert mat into frame; secure frame backing.

SCRAPBOOKING BOXES

Turn castoff containers into scrapbook heaven — in no time at all! Choose a variety of boxes big enough to hold stickers, mounting squares, paper scraps, and other materials. Embellish with coordinating fabric, matching ribbon, and orphaned buttons. Your friends will turn green with envy!

COVERED BOXES

Recycled items: four graduated-size boxes with lids, fabric pieces, and assorted buttons

You will also need spray adhesive, hot glue gun, and ribbon.

Use hot glue gun for all gluing unless otherwise indicated.

1. For each box, cut a piece of fabric large enough to cover box. Center box on wrong side of fabric and draw around box.

2. Use ruler to draw lines ¹/₂" outside drawn lines, extending lines to edges of fabric. Draw diagonal lines from intersections of outer lines to corners of original lines.

3. Cut away corners of fabric and clip along diagonal lines (Fig. 1).

Fig. 1

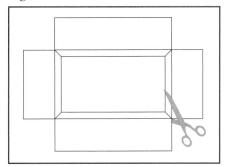

4. Apply spray adhesive to wrong side of fabric.

5. Center box on fabric, matching box to original drawn lines; smooth fabric on bottom of box.

6. To cover front and back of box, smooth fabric onto front and back sides of box. Smooth excess fabric around corners onto adjacent sides. Smooth fabric to inside of box, clipping as necessary (Fig. 2).

Fig. 2

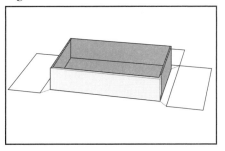

7. To cover each end, smooth fabric onto end of box. Trim excess fabric even with corners. Smooth fabric to inside of box.

8. Follow the technique in Steps 1 – 7 to cover each lid.

9. Referring to Fig. 3, glue lengths of ribbon to each box and lid.

Fig. 3

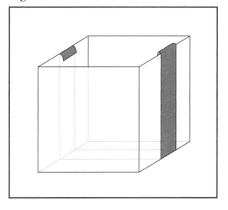

10. For each lid, cut a piece of ribbon 2" long; fold into a loop and glue ends together. Aligning loop with ribbon on lid, glue to inside front edge of lid. Stack and glue large, then small buttons to ribbon on lip of box.

11. For bow, cut a length of ribbon and glue ends of ribbon to center, making two loops; glue bow to ribbon on top box. Glue button to center of bow.

ELEGANT ACCENT TABLE

Stately pillars and winding vines make this timeless table reminiscent of something from Caesar's palace. No one will ever guess it's created from recycled trash! Construct columns from coffee cans, children's swimming "noodles," and an old garden hose. Graceful "ivy" is made from aluminum cans and floral wire. Uncanny!

COFFEE CAN TABLE AND SODA-CAN VINE

Recycled items: nine same-size large coffee cans with lids, large wallpaper scraps, garden hose, two swimming noodles (cut in half lengthwise), six wire clothes hangers, natural sponges, large felt scraps, aluminum beverage cans, and craft foam

You will also need sand, duct tape, spray adhesive, utility scissors, miter box and saw, hot glue gun, wire cutters, brown spray primer, pre-mixed spackle compound, putty knife, stone-colored spray texture paint, white gesso, light brown and gold acrylic paint, matte clear acrylic spray sealer, self-adhesive rubber surface protectors, tracing paper, stylus, pushpin, floral wire, green spray paint, and tempered glass for tabletop.

Refer to Painting Techniques, page 151, before beginning project. Allow adhesive, primer, spackle, paint, and sealer to dry after each application.

COLUMNS

1. (*Note:* Using three cans, follow Steps 1 – 7 to make each column.) Fill bottom can with sand to weight. Place lids on cans. Stack and tape cans together.

2. Measure height of column; measure circumference of column and add $1/2$". Cut a piece of wallpaper the determined measurements. Apply spray adhesive to wrong side of wallpaper piece; overlapping at back of column, smooth paper around column. Tape seam to secure.

3. Cut two lengths of hose and noodle halves to fit around column. Using miter box and cutting ends in same direction, cut each hose and noodle end at a 45-degree angle.

4. Glue noodle halves around top and bottom of column; tape seams.

5. Thread hanger through hose length and form a loop at one end; wrap around column just above noodle and thread end of wire through loop. Pull wire to tighten, then fold end of wire around itself to secure. Trim excess wire and cover seam with tape. Turn column over and repeat Steps 5 and 6 along top edge.

6. Apply primer to column. Randomly apply spackle to column, filling any gaps and adding texture. Apply texture paint to column, then *Sponge Paint* using a mixture of three parts gesso and one part brown paint. Apply sealer to column.

7. Glue a piece of felt over bottom of column; attach surface protectors to top of column for glass to sit on.

VINE

1. Cutting through openings in cans, cut down side of each can to bottom rim. Cut away and discard tops and bottoms of cans; flatten remaining pieces.

2. Trace leaf patterns, page 132, onto tracing paper; cut out. Draw around patterns on can pieces; cut out leaves (we cut out fifteen leaves of each size).

3. To emboss each leaf, place leaf on craft foam. Use stylus to draw veins on leaf. Use pushpin to punch hole in base of leaf.

4. Cut a 4" length of floral wire for each leaf. Thread wire through hole in leaf and loop at back; glue to secure.

5. Attach leaves to floral wire every 3- to 4-inches, coiling stems and alternating sides and lengths of wire. Cut several 4" pieces of wire and wrap around pencil to coil; attach to vine.

6. Apply primer to vine and paint green; *Dry Brush* gold. Apply sealer to vine.

7. Wrap vine around columns and place glass on top of columns.

PHOTOGRAPHER'S MYSTERY COLLAGE

*W*here in the world was THAT taken? If you've amassed lots of unidentified photos, it may be time to combine those misfits into a clever collage. Brown paper bags become a travel-worn backdrop, while upholstery tacks and paper corners hold photos in place. Friends will love your mysterious conversation piece!

BROWN PAPER FRAME

Recycled items: two 17" x 27" pieces of corrugated cardboard, photographs, brown paper bags, thin aluminum oven liner, natural sponge, and a greeting card with globe motif

You will also need utility scissors, multicolored ink pad, embossing powder, blow dryer, rubber stamp (we used a postmark stamp), craft glue, tape, stylus, paintbrushes, green and cream acrylic paint, hot glue gun, and upholstery tacks.

Refer to Painting Techniques, page 151, before beginning project. Use craft glue for all gluing unless otherwise indicated.

1. Cut opening in one piece of cardboard for frame. Secure photos to remaining piece to show in frame.

2. Crumple, then flatten enough brown paper to cover frame. Working in small sections, run ink pad over paper. While ink is wet, sprinkle paper with embossing powder; remove excess powder. Repeat process for entire piece of paper. Using blow dryer, heat powder until melted.

3. Stamp paper as desired. Tear paper into small pieces and glue to frame, covering completely.

4. For phrase, enlarge pattern, page 132, to fit on frame. Tape pattern to oven liner; draw over lines on pattern with stylus to emboss. Remove pattern.

5. Cut out phrase; paint right side green, then *Sponge Paint* green for texture. While paint is tacky, use stylus to lightly draw over right side of words to remove paint.

6. Paint inside of letters cream. Using hot glue, adhere phrase to frame, then adhere frame to backing.

7. Secure photos to frame using upholstery tacks and decorative photo corners (we cut globes from a card into quarters).

EYE-CATCHING OUTDOOR CHARM

*P*rettify your porch with an exquisite outdoor accent. Old brooches, mismatched earrings, discarded charms, and other spangles are just right for creating your own one-of-a-kind bauble. Go for an elegant, golden appearance or a colorful, funky look — whatever strikes your fancy!

OUTDOOR JEWELRY DECORATION

Recycled items: jewelry (we used a brooch, chain links, jump rings, earrings, bracelets, charms, and jewelry clasps)

You will also need needle-nose pliers.

1. Remove pin from brooch.

2. Use chain links or jump rings to secure earrings, bracelets, and charms to brooch.

3. For hanger, attach clasps to the ends of a length of necklace or bracelet; secure one end to top of brooch.

FISHIN' FOR PHOTOS

*O*ur fisherman's photo display is a "reel" catch! Form the fishing pole base from extra-long cardboard tubes. A candy tin, a canned fruit container, and cast-off lids are just the right size for showing off favorite photos. Finish by stringing up a cute aluminum can fish.

CARDBOARD FISHING POLE

Recycled items: two cardboard gift wrap tubes, newspaper, five aluminum can tabs, felt scraps, $1\frac{1}{2}$"w ribbon spool, toothbrush, three black pen caps, and a black pen body

You will also need utility scissors; hot glue gun; découpage glue; primer; black and silver spray paint; paintbrushes; red, gold, and black acrylic paint; and fishing line.

Use hot glue for all gluing unless otherwise indicated. Allow primer, glue, and paint to dry after each application.

1. For pole, cut cardboard tubes in half lengthwise. Twist one tube, making a point at one end; glue to hold shape. Repeat for second tube, inserting pointed end of tube into large end of first tube; glue to secure.

2. Tear newspaper into strips and place in water to soak for several hours. Remove strips from water and squeeze excess water from strips. Dip strips in découpage glue and cover pole in the opposite direction of the twist until a smooth surface is achieved.

3. Apply primer to pole, then spray paint black.

4. For rings, bend can tabs in half; referring to Fig. 1 and spacing as desired, glue rings to pole. Paint a red stripe around pole on each side of rings. Outline red stripes with gold.

Fig. 1

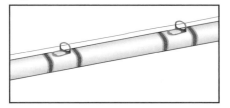

5. Leaving space for reel, glue a piece of felt around end of pole for handle.

6. For reel, apply primer to spool; paint silver, then *Spatter Paint,* page 152, black. Referring to Handle Diagram, use pen caps and pen body to construct handle, then glue handle into hole of spool. Glue reel to pole.

7. Wrap reel with fishing line and run line through rings; knot line to last ring.

HANDLE DIAGRAM

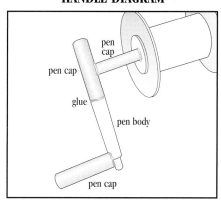

pen cap

pen cap

glue

pen body

pen cap

RECYCLED FRAMES

Recycled items: small hinged metal tin, photographs, fishing lure, $3^{1}/_{4}$" dia. can with top removed, corrugated cardboard, mesh bag, plastic take-out tray, bumps cut from plastic lemon-lime soda bottle, paper clip, $3^{3}/_{4}$" dia. plastic lid, natural sponge pieces, and a pushpin

You will also need white spray primer, hot glue gun, fishing line, hammer and awl, craft knife and cutting mat, and black spray paint.

Allow primer and paint to dry after each application. Use a dab of hot glue to secure knots in fishing line as needed.

HINGED-TIN FRAME

1. Apply primer to the outside of tin. Draw around tin on photo; cut out just inside drawn line. Secure photo in lid and glue lure in tin.

2. To hang frame from Cardboard Fishing Pole, knot a length of fishing line around pole and glue line at back of pole to secure. Knot line around top hinge of tin and glue at back to secure.

31

TIN CAN FRAME

1. Use hammer and awl to make two holes centered in the side of the can ¼" apart. Thread a length of fishing line through holes in tin and knot to secure.

2. Draw around can on cardboard four times and once on photo; cut out circles just inside drawn lines. Set one cardboard circle aside. Stack and glue cardboard circles inside can; secure photo to circles. Place mesh bag around can and glue remaining cardboard circle to back of can to secure bag in place.

3. To hang frame from Cardboard Fishing Pole, page 30, knot a length of fishing line around pole and glue line at back of pole to secure.

PLASTIC LINER FRAME

1. Cut a frame from take-out tray with an opening slightly smaller than a 4" x 6" photo. Prime, then paint frame and bumps cut from bottle black. Secure photo to a cardboard backing cut slightly larger than photo; glue to frame. Decorate frame with bumps.

2. To hang frame from Cardboard Fishing Pole, page 30, knot a length of fishing line around the pole and glue line at back of pole to secure. Tie and knot line to paper clip; glue paper clip to backing.

PLASTIC LID FRAME

1. Draw around lid on photo; cut out just inside drawn line. Secure photo in lid. Glue sponge pieces to rim of lid.

2. To hang frame from Cardboard Fishing Pole, page 30, knot a length of fishing line around pole and glue line at back of pole to secure. Use pushpin to make a hole at top of lid; thread line through hole and knot on inside of lid to secure.

"Recycled" picture frames also look great in a mantel grouping. Display one on an easel for added interest.

CARDBOARD STANDS FOR FRAMES

Recycled items: corrugated cardboard

You will also need utility scissors, and craft glue.

1. For backing, cut a 2" x 6" piece from cardboard. Refer to Fig. 1 to score stand.

Fig. 1

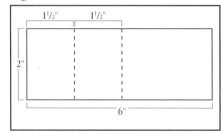

2. Referring to Fig. 2, fold stand and glue to back of frame.

Fig. 2

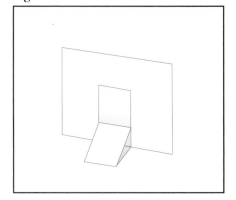

SODA-CAN TROUT

Recycled items: a 12-oz. aluminum beverage can, natural sponge, and a pushpin

You will need utility scissors; spray primer; black and green spray paint; tracing paper; light-colored craft foam; decorative-edged craft scissors; paintbrushes; yellow, green, orange, pink, brown, tan, white, and black acrylic paint; household cement; matte clear acrylic spray sealer; fishing line; and a hot glue gun.

Refer to Painting Techniques, page 151, before beginning project. Use cement for all gluing unless otherwise indicated. Allow primer, paint, household cement, and sealer to dry after each application.

1. Cut top from can. For mouth, squeeze opening into an oval shape. Apply primer to inside and outside of can. Spray paint inside of can black.

2. Trace fin patterns, page 133, onto tracing paper; cut out. Draw around patterns on craft foam; cut out. Use craft scissors to trim curved edges of dorsal fin and tail fin. Spray paint both sides of pectoral fins and outside of can green.

3. Paint rim of can, pectoral fin, and tail fin yellow. Follow *Sponge Painting* to paint curved edges of dorsal fin and tail fin green. Paint yellow and orange details on both sides of pectoral fins. Glue dorsal fin and tail fin to can.

4. *Sponge Paint* belly of fish yellow, area under mouth orange, and a pink stripe along each side of fish. Paint brown, tan, and orange *Dots* on sides of fish, then smaller orange *Dots* over several brown dots. Paint white eyes with black pupils; add yellow highlights.

Impress your fishing buddies with a string of funny soda-can fish.

5. Glue pectoral fins to sides of fish. Apply two to three coats of sealer to fish.

6. To hang fish from Cardboard Fishing Pole, page 30, knot a length of fishing line around pole and hot glue line at back of pole to secure. Use pushpin to make a hole at top of mouth. Thread a length of line through hole; knot line on inside of fish and hot glue to secure.

STRINGER OF FISH

You will need a pushpin, paper clips or safety pins, and a stringer or length of chain.

1. Follow Steps 1 – 5 of Soda-Can Trout, to make three fish.

2. Use pushpin to make a hole at top of mouth of each fish. Use paper clip to attach fish to stringer.

soft and simple

Time-worn tablecloths, cast-off jeans, and fabric scraps are easily transformed into crafty creations for everyday use. From a smart pillow set and cozy rag rugs to a lovable lamb and a handy organizer for sewing supplies, every easy project is sure to please. These and other fun fabric designs are pretty, practical, and oh-so soft.

SOOTHING EYE BUTTERFLY

*F*loat off in daydreams while moist heat or soothing coolness refreshes and revitalizes tired eyes. Our butterfly mask pampers your face with a scrap of soft fabric and an old vinyl tablecloth. Fill with rice, zap in the microwave or cool in the freezer, and you're ready to relax!

TABLECLOTH EYE SOOTHER

Recycled items: a vinyl flannel-backed tablecloth, large clear plastic take-out container, and a fabric scrap

You will also need tracing paper, craft knife and cutting mat, stencil brushes and sponges, assorted colors of acrylic paint, fabric glue, rice, and black embroidery floss.

1. Trace outer line of butterfly pattern, page 133, onto tracing paper. Pin tracing paper to tablecloth, and using pattern, cut out two butterflies.

2. For stencil, trace entire butterfly pattern onto container; use craft knife to cut out grey areas. Draw around stencil on fabric.

3. To stencil design onto fabric, dip a dry stencil brush or sponge into paint; remove excess paint on a paper towel. For best results, brush or sponge should be almost dry. Beginning at edge of cutout area, apply paint in a stamping motion over stencil. If desired, highlight or shade design by stamping a lighter or darker shade of paint in cutout area. Repeat until all areas of stencil are painted. Use brush to paint designs on butterfly. Cut out fabric butterfly.

4. Matching fleece sides and leaving an opening for filling, glue along inside edges of tablecloth pieces 1/4" from edge. Fill each wing with 1 1/2 tablespoons of rice; glue opening closed. Pin fabric butterfly to one side of eye soother. Referring to Butterfly Diagram and using three strands of floss, work *Running Stitches*, page 153, to form body; work *Blanket Stitches* along edges of eye soother.

BUTTERFLY DIAGRAM

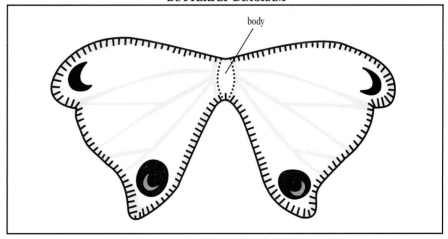

Tip: When freezing, place mask in a resealable plastic bag. To heat mask, begin heating for one minute in microwave. Continue heating at 15 second intervals, if necessary, to reach desired heat.

KEEN JEAN BOLSTER

Groovy old "threads" can really bolster your home fashion scene! A worn-out jeans leg is a "hip" covering for a clever pillow made from packing peanuts, bubble wrap, and a 3-liter bottle. Cut-off seams tie things up, while a patterned bandanna tucked in a transplanted pocket offers a casual accent.

DENIM BOLSTER PILLOW

Recycled items: a 3-liter plastic beverage bottle, foam packing peanuts, bubble wrap, denim jeans (leg must be large enough to accommodate the 3-liter bottle), and a bandanna

You will also need packing tape and fabric glue.

1. Fill bottle with foam peanuts and replace cap. Cover bottle with bubble wrap; secure with tape.

2. Cut a 24^1/$_2$" long piece from jeans leg; hem raw edges. Center bottle inside tube.

3. For ties, cut flat-fold seams from jeans; knot ties around pillow at ends of bottle.

4. Cut pocket from jeans. Gluing along side and bottom edges, attach pocket to pillow; allow to dry. Tuck a piece of bandanna in pocket.

LOVABLE LAMB

*C*hildren and adults alike will treasure our enchanting little lamb. Chenille scrap "wool," a sock face, and felt hooves make this fuzzy friend oh-so soft to touch. What a "be-ewe-tiful" baby!

CHENILLE AND SOCK SCRAPS LAMB

Recycled items: one tan and one pink baby sock, chenille scraps, and brown felt scraps

You will also need polyester fiberfill, tracing paper, and fabric glue.

Match right sides and use a ¹⁄₄" seam allowance for all sewing.

1. For face, stuff toe of tan sock half full with fiberfill.

2. For body, cut a 9" x 13" piece of chenille; press short edges ¹⁄₂" to wrong side. Sew long edges together to form a tube.

3. Work *Running Stitches*, page 153, along short edges of each end of body. Insert stuffed sock into one end of body; pull thread to gather around sock (Fig. 1). Stitch in place to secure. Turn body right side out.

Fig. 1

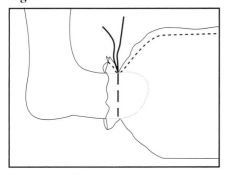

4. Stuff tube with fiberfill, pull threads tight, then knot to secure.

5. Trace ear/tail, inner ear, and hoof patterns, page 134, onto tracing paper. Use patterns to cut six ear/tail pieces from chenille, two inner ear pieces from pink sock, and eight hooves from brown felt.

6. For each ear/tail, place two chenille pieces together; leaving straight edges open, sew pieces together. Turn ear/tail right side out and turn raw edges ¹⁄₄" to inside. For each ear, position an inner ear piece on chenille ear. Turning raw edges under, hand sew inner ear to chenille ear.

7. To shape each ear/tail, pinch straight end of ear/tail together and glue to lamb. Tack edges to secure.

8. Leaving straight edges open, sew hoof pieces together. Turn right side out and stuff lightly with fiberfill.

9. For each leg, cut a 2" x 5" piece from chenille; fold one long edge ¹⁄₄" to wrong side and stitch in place. Sew short ends together to form tube; turn right side out. Insert hoof ¹⁄₄" in finished end of leg; hand sew to secure. Work *Running Stitches* along top edge of leg; pull threads to gather ends and knot to secure.

10. Sew legs to bottom of body.

BLOOMING COMFORTS

Mom's old tablecloth has never looked so good! Start with big blocks of color, then add lively vintage accents. Or go for a muted look with vibrant blossoms blooming from softly textured dishtowels. Finish with bedsheet backings, leftover fringe, and cording.

TABLECLOTH PILLOWS

Recycled items: a fabric tablecloth with motifs and a border, two colors of waffle weave kitchen towels to coordinate with tablecloth (one for each pillow and one for each background), fringe, and a sheet

You will also need heavy-duty fusible web, pillow form, cording, hot glue gun, and polyester fiberfill.

SMALL PILLOW WITH CORDING TRIM

1. Using a motif cut from tablecloth, follow *Fusible Appliqués*, page 153, to make appliqué. Fuse appliqué to background towel.

2. Cut background towel $1/2$" outside of appliqué edges. Pin background towel on one end of pillow cover towel, then zigzag stitch along edges of background towel.

3. For pillow cover, fold towel in half, then place pillow form between towel layers. Sew along sides and bottom of pillow form, leaving cover edges open.

4. Knot one end of a length of cording, then use hot glue to secure cording along side and bottom seams of cover; knot and trim remaining end.

SMALL PILLOW WITH FRINGE TRIM

1. Matching short ends of pillow cover towel, fold towel in half and cut apart along fold.

2. Cut a square from background towel (square should fit center of pillow front and leave room for border trim).

3. Using a motif cut from tablecloth, follow *Fusible Appliqués* to make appliqué. Fuse appliqué to background square. Fold edges of square under $1/4$"; pin square to pillow front, then sew along edges.

4. Using two border strips cut from tablecloth, follow *Fusible Appliqués* to make appliqués. Fuse to pillow front on each side of background square.

5. Pin fringe along right side edges of one pillow cover piece. With right sides matching and leaving an opening for stuffing, sew along edges through all layers.

6. Turn cover right side out and stuff with fiberfill. Sew opening closed.

7. Hot glue cording along background square $1/4$" inside edges.

GREEN TABLECLOTH PILLOW

Match right sides and use a $1/2$" seam allowance for all sewing.

1. Centering motif, cut a piece of tablecloth desired size for pillow front; cut accents from border to fit on corners of pillow front. Using accents, follow *Fusible Appliqués* to make appliqués, then fuse to corners of pillow front.

2. For pillow back, cut a piece from sheet the same size as pillow front.

3. Leaving an opening for stuffing, sew front and back together.

4. Turn pillow right side out; stuff with fiberfill. Sew opening closed.

VINTAGE VOGUE SHIRT

Dress up a denim shirt with a few feminine flourishes. Scraps of patchwork add cheerful splashes of color, and a fanciful handkerchief makes a dainty accent. Fashion extra-sweet oversized pockets from an embroidered dresser scarf. How positively darling!

VINTAGE FABRIC-EMBELLISHED SHIRT

Recycled items: a denim shirt, dresser scarf with embroidered ends for appliquéd pockets (scarf should be about the same width as one side of shirt front), assorted buttons, quilt top scrap, fabric scrap, and a vintage handkerchief

You will also need heavy-duty thread and tracing paper.

Refer to Pattern Diagram while making project. Use ¹/₂" seam allowance for all sewing unless otherwise indicated.

1. Place shirt flat on work surface.

2. For appliquéd pockets, cut scarf in half width wise. For each pocket, pin one scarf half on shirt front with decorative edge at top. Cut bottom edge ¹/₂" past bottom of shirt. Remove scarf from shirt and press raw edges ¹/₂" to wrong side.

3. Repin pockets on shirt. Mark a vertical seam line down center of each pocket. Sew along side and bottom edges of pockets, then sew a seam along each side of vertical seam lines; sew a button at top of each vertical seam.

4. For collar embellishment, use shirt as a guide and refer to Pattern Diagram to make separate patterns on tracing paper for collar and band; use patterns to cut collar piece from quilt scrap and band piece from fabric scrap.

5. Matching right sides and raw edges, sew bottom edge of collar piece to top edge of band piece; press seam allowance toward band. Press remaining raw edges of band piece ¹/₄" to wrong side. Pin embellishment to collar and top stitch in place. Zigzag stitch along outer edges of collar.

6. For sleeve bands, cut a 1"w strip of quilt scrap to fit around sleeve edge; pin band around sleeve. Zigzag stitch along edges of band.

7. Sew a button to shirt pocket. Place handkerchief in pocket.

PATTERN DIAGRAM

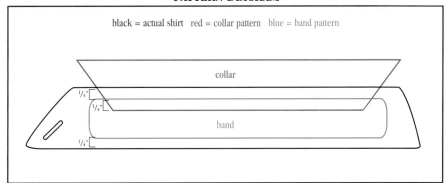

black = actual shirt   red = collar pattern   blue = band pattern

collar

¹/₄"

¹/₄"

band

¹/₄"

TEA TIME VEST

*F*ashion this tasteful "tea party" vest from a discarded bed coverlet! Adorn the panels with sweet motifs cut from a kitchen towel, and enhance the edge with lacy trim. How perfectly "tea-lightful!"

APPLIQUÉD COVERLET VEST

Recycled items: a vest pattern, coverlet, kitchen towels with same motifs and borders, and scraps of trim

You will also need heavy-duty paper-backed fusible web, rotary cutter with wavy-edged blade and cutting mat, and clear nylon thread.

1. Using vest pattern, make vest from coverlet. For pocket, cut a square from coverlet; hem edges and sew to vest.

2. Fuse web to wrong side of towels; do not remove paper backing. Using rotary cutter, cut out borders. Cut motifs from towels; arrange and fuse appliqués on vest.

3. Stitch trim in place along bottom edge of vest. Fuse towel border above trim.

4. Use clear thread to stitch appliqués in place.

PRIORITY PAPERWEIGHTS

K*eep your priorities in check with handsome "pillow" paperweights. Made with weathered leather from an old jacket or handbag, these sand-filled weights are the essence of understated sophistication. Stylish gold-stamped words designate levels of urgency and remind you of looming deadlines.*

LEATHER PAPERWEIGHTS

Recycled items: a leather jacket or bag and sand

You will also need utility scissors, alphabet rubber stamps, gold ink pad, paper towels, matte clear acrylic spray sealer, and a heavy-duty needle and thread.

Use a $1/4$" seam allowance for all sewing.

1. For each paperweight, cut two 6" squares from leather.

2. Using alphabet stamps, stamp desired words on right side of one square; blot excess with paper towel. Apply sealer and allow to dry.

3. Matching right sides and leaving an opening for turning and filling, sew squares together; clip corners, then turn right side out.

4. Fill bag with sand and sew opening closed.

Keep your sewing supplies in the bag! Coordinating placemats form the shell of this nifty needlework organizer, while resealable plastic bags store odds and ends for sewing, crafting, or other hobbies. Choose bags of various shapes and sizes to custom-fit your needs.

PLACEMAT NEEDLEWORK ORGANIZER

Recycled items: two double-sided fabric placemats, fabric, assorted resealable plastic bags, 1½" x 5" strip of thin packing foam sheet, and a piece of cording

You will also need a fabric marking pen, two ⅜" dia. grommets and a grommet setter, and two hook and loop fasteners.

1. Draw around one placemat on fabric; cut out shape ½" outside drawn line. Press fabric edges ½" to wrong side.

2. Arranging bags as desired, sew along side and bottom edges of plastic bags to attach bags to right side of fabric piece. Tack packing foam in place.

3. Matching wrong sides, fold one placemat in half. Matching edges, place folded mat on right side of remaining mat; match folded edge to end of mat. Unfold mat and pin mats together. Sew mats together along side seams and along edges of bottom mat where mats overlap (Fig 1). Sewing through all layers, sew fabric piece to top mat along all edges.

Fig. 1

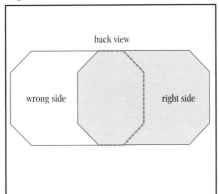

back view

wrong side   right side

4. Referring to Fig. 2, mark placement for grommets; follow manufacturer's instructions to attach grommets.

Fig. 2

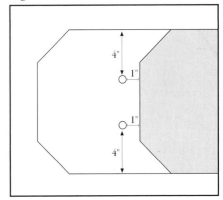

5. For handle, insert ends of cording through grommets to inside of organizer; knot to secure.

6. Aligning fasteners to connect, sew hook pieces to inside of top flap and loop pieces to outside of bottom flap.

HANDY BAG HANGER

*H*old it right there! A lively checkered tablecloth is transformed into a clever organizer, perfect for putting away plastic shopping bags, pantyhose, socks, or other lightweight items. Trim this helpful hanging bag with leftover rickrack and colorful buttons.

HANGING STORAGE BAG

Recycled items: a plastic clothes hanger, fabric tablecloth, and coordinating buttons

You will also need fabric glue and jumbo rickrack.

1. To make pattern, lay hanger on a piece of paper. Refer to Fig. 1 to draw around top and sides of hanger, then extend sides to desired length for bag. Cut out pattern.

Fig. 1

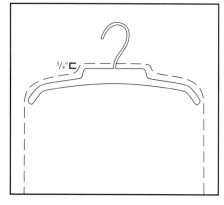

2. Draw around pattern twice on wrong side of tablecloth; cut out ¹/₂" outside drawn lines. Cut a horizontal opening in one piece, just below bottom of hanger; fold raw edges of opening ¹/₄" to wrong side and glue to secure.

3. With right sides together, using a ¹/₂" seam allowance and leaving an opening at center top for inserting hook of hanger, sew pieces together. Turn bag right side out.

4. Beginning and ending at center back, glue rickrack around bag along lower edge of opening. Attach buttons to rickrack, then carefully place hanger inside bag.

"Can-Do" Pin Cushion

*O*ur quaint catch-all makes a handy sewing companion. Flowered fabric from an old tablecloth covers a pull-top can, providing the perfect place to store sewing supplies or other notions. Leftover foam core holds a pretty pin cushion lid in place.

PIN CUSHION-TOPPED CAN NOTIONS HOLDER

Recycled items: pull-top can (such as a soup or fruit can), tablecloth, heavy-weight cardboard (we used the back of a writing tablet), and a foam core scrap

You will also need fusible fleece, hot glue gun, fabric glue, ribbon, polyester fiberfill, and two sizes of rickrack.

Use fabric glue for all gluing unless otherwise indicated.

1. Measure around can and add $1/2$"; measure height of can and add 1". Cut a piece from tablecloth using determined measurements, then cut a strip of fleece the same size as can measurements. Center and fuse fleece to wrong side of tablecloth piece; press edges $1/2$" to wrong side. Hot glue tablecloth piece to can; glue ribbon around bottom of can.

2. For lid, draw around bottom of can onto cardboard, tablecloth, and foam core. Cut out cardboard circle $1/2$" outside drawn line, cut out tablecloth 1" outside drawn line, then cut out foam core just inside drawn line.

3. Center cardboard circle on wrong side of tablecloth circle; clip fabric edges $1/4$". Wrap edges to back of cardboard and hot glue clipped edges in place, leaving a 1" opening for stuffing with fiberfill. Insert fiberfill, then hot glue opening closed. Hot glue foam core circle to bottom of lid.

4. Glue large rickrack along underside edge of lid; glue small rickrack along top edge of lid.

RUGGED RAG RUGS

Indulge your feet with cozy rag rugs. Made from narrow strips of old jeans and chambray work shirts, these handsome rugs are a snap to crochet. Strips of different colors create eye-catching patterns.

CROCHETED RUGS

SCRAP OVAL RUG

FINISHED SIZE: 27" x 38"
(68.5 cm x 96.5 cm)

Recycled Items: denim and/or chambray clothing

You will also need a crochet hook, size P (10 mm)

Read Crochet Basics, page 154, before beginning project.

Prepare fabric and cut into ³/₄" strips (19 mm).

Ch 22 loosely.

Rnd 1 (Right side)**:** Sc in second ch from hook and in each ch across to last ch, 3 sc in last ch; working in free loops of beginning ch (Fig. 1, page 154), sc in next 19 chs, 2 sc in next ch; join with slip st to first sc: 44 sc.

Rnd 2: Ch 1, 2 sc in same st, sc in next 19 sc, 2 sc in each of next 3 sc, sc in next 19 sc, 2 sc in each of last 2 sc; join with slip st to first sc: 50 sc.

Rnd 3: Ch 1, sc in same st, 2 sc in next sc, sc in next 20 sc, 2 sc in next sc, (sc in next sc, 2 sc in next sc) twice, sc in next 20 sc, 2 sc in next sc, sc in next sc, 2 sc in next sc; join with slip st to first sc: 56 sc.

Rnd 4: Ch 1, 2 sc in same st, sc in next sc, 2 sc in next sc, sc in next 21 sc, 2 sc in next sc, (sc in next sc, 2 sc in next sc) 3 times, sc in next 21 sc, (2 sc in next sc, sc in next sc) twice; join with slip st to first sc: 64 sc.

Rnd 5: Ch 1, sc in same st and in next sc, 2 sc in next sc, sc in next 25 sc, 2 sc in next sc, (sc in next 2 sc, 2 sc in next sc) twice, sc in next 25 sc, 2 sc in next sc, sc in next 2 sc, 2 sc in last sc; join with slip st to first sc: 70 sc.

Rnd 6: Ch 1, 2 sc in same st, sc in next 2 sc, 2 sc in next sc, sc in next 25 sc, 2 sc in next sc, (sc in next 2 sc, 2 sc in next sc) 3 times, sc in next 25 sc, (2 sc in next sc, sc in next 2 sc) twice; join with slip st to first sc: 78 sc.

Rnd 7: Ch 1, sc in same st and in next 2 sc, 2 sc in next sc, sc in next 28 sc, 2 sc in next sc, (sc in next 4 sc, 2 sc in next sc) twice, sc in next 28 sc, 2 sc in next sc, sc in next 4 sc, 2 sc in next sc, sc in last sc; join with slip st to first sc: 84 sc.

Rnd 8: Ch 1, sc in same st, 2 sc in next sc, sc in next 4 sc, 2 sc in next sc, sc in next 26 sc, 2 sc in next sc, (sc in next 4 sc, 2 sc in next sc) 3 times, sc in next 26 sc, 2 sc in next sc, sc in next 4 sc, 2 sc in next sc, sc in last 3 sc; join with slip st to first sc: 92 sc.

Rnd 9: Ch 1, sc in same st and in next 4 sc, 2 sc in next sc, sc in next 33 sc, 2 sc in next sc, (sc in next 5 sc, 2 sc in next sc) twice, sc in next 33 sc, 2 sc in next sc, sc in next 5 sc, 2 sc in last sc; join with slip st to first sc: 98 sc.

Rnd 10: Ch 1, sc in same st and in next sc, 2 sc in next sc, sc in next 6 sc, 2 sc in next sc, sc in next 27 sc, 2 sc in next sc, (sc in next 6 sc, 2 sc in next sc) 3 times, sc in next 27 sc, 2 sc in next sc, sc in next 6 sc, 2 sc in next sc, sc in last 4 sc; join with slip st to first sc: 106 sc.

Rnd 11: Ch 1, sc in same st and in next 5 sc, 2 sc in next sc, sc in next 38 sc, 2 sc in next sc, (sc in next 6 sc, 2 sc in next sc) twice, sc in next 38 sc, 2 sc in next sc, sc in next 6 sc, 2 sc in last sc; join with slip st to first sc: 112 sc.

Rnd 12: Ch 1, sc in same st and in next sc, 2 sc in next sc, sc in next 7 sc, 2 sc in next sc, sc in next 31 sc, 2 sc in next sc, (sc in next 7 sc, 2 sc in next sc) 3 times, sc in next 31 sc, 2 sc in next sc, sc in next 7 sc, 2 sc in next sc, sc in last 5 sc; join with slip st to first sc: 120 sc.

Rnd 13: Ch 1, sc in same st and in next 6 sc, 2 sc in next sc, sc in next 43 sc, 2 sc in next sc, (sc in next 7 sc, 2 sc in next sc) twice, sc in next 43 sc, 2 sc in next sc, sc in next 7 sc, 2 sc in last sc; join with slip st to first sc: 126 sc.

(continued on page 155)

1. Feed cat
2. Clean your room
3. Wash dishes

creative touches

Distinctive accents made from ordinary "trash" add a little something special to your home and garden. Turn empty coffee cans into "de-light-ful" luminaries. Transform a cardboard container and shredded paper into a decorator accent. Find new uses for broken china and disposable aluminum pans. The creative touches on the following pages will inspire you to turn your trash into tasteful décor.

FLOATING FLOWER CANDLES

*D*elicate candle posies make a refreshing water garden. Just refashion old candles into flowery shapes using plastic bottle molds. For a beautiful blossoming effect, try stacking large and small flowers.

FLOATING FLOWER CANDLES

Recycled items: 1-liter and 3-liter plastic beverage bottles, dripless taper and pillar candles, and large metal cans

You will also need a utility knife, wax colorant (if desired), and cooking spray.

1. For molds, cut bottoms from bottles.

2. For each flower candle, cut a 2" piece from wick end of taper candle or cut a 3" piece from center of taper and cut away one end to expose wick. For flower petals, cut remaining candles into small pieces.

3. For each petal color, follow *Melting Wax*, page 152, and place candle pieces in can to melt.

4. Coat molds with cooking spray.

5. For large flower petals, pour melted wax into 3-liter molds; allow to harden. For flower candles, pour melted wax for petals into 1-liter molds and allow to partially harden; insert taper candle pieces into centers of petals, then allow to harden completely. Remove petals and candles from molds. Invert large flower petals and place flower candles on top.

PERKY PLANT POKES

*P*layful plant markers are a clever way to identify the flowers and "weeds" in your garden. Turn aluminum cans into pretty posies with scissors, paint, and whimsical rubber stamps. Attach these frolicsome flowers to driftwood for a delightful look.

ALUMINUM CAN FLOWER PLANT POKES

Recycled items: 12-oz. aluminum beverage cans, toothbrush, and pieces of driftwood

You will also need repositionable spray adhesive; utility scissors; rust-colored spray primer; paintbrushes; brown, yellow, green, and other desired colors of acrylic paint; spouncer; alphabet rubber stamps; assorted colors of ink pads; clear acrylic spray sealer; coarse sandpaper; tack cloth; and hammer and ⁵/₈"-long finishing nails.

Follow Painting Techniques, page 151, before beginning project. Allow primer, paint, ink, and sealer to dry after each application.

1. For each flower, enlarge desired petal pattern strip, page 135, 118%; cut out. Apply adhesive to wrong side of strip; allow to dry until tacky to touch. Adhere strip around bottom of can. Cutting through opening in can, cut down side of can to top cutting line. Cut bottom from can along top line of strip. Discard top of can.

2. Cut around petals and remove pattern; bend petals outward.

3. Prime, then paint each flower; *Spatter Paint* flower brown. Use spouncer to *Sponge Paint* center of flower yellow. Stamp name of flower in center. Apply sealer to front of flower to seal name.

4. Paint driftwood piece with a watery mixture of green paint. Lightly sand driftwood, allowing bare wood to show through; wipe with tack cloth. Nail flower to driftwood piece through flower center; paint nail head green. Apply sealer to flowers.

GLORIOUS GARDEN ANGELS

*E*nhance your yard with angelic plant pokes. Disposable aluminum pans embossed with household items give these angels old-time appeal, while wings made from decorative household hardware keep them on cloud nine. Painted to match the hues of your garden, these plant pokes will dress up any flowerbed.

ALUMINUM ANGEL PLANT POKES

Recycled items: a large paint stir stick (ours measure ¼" x 1½" x 21"), disassembled wooden clothespin, disposable aluminum pan, small nail, items to emboss aluminum (we used nuts, bolts, screws, and chains), items for wings (we used an outlet cover, two decorative drawer plates, and a decorative wooden piece), white wire clothes hanger, and a spiral wire from a notebook

You will also need black and desired color of spray paint, paintbrush, white acrylic paint, sandpaper, tack cloth, drill and ¹⁄₃₂" bit, utility scissors, stylus, hammer, rust-colored spray primer, wire cutters, rusted craft wire, staple gun, household cement, and pliers.

Allow paint, primer, and household cement to dry after each application.

1. For each body, paint stir stick and clothespin pieces black, then paint white. Lightly sand pieces to allow black to show through; wipe with tack cloth.

2. Refer to Fig. 1 to drill a hole through each clothespin piece.

Fig. 1

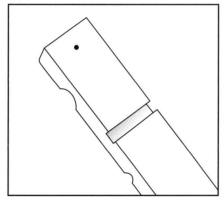

3. For each dress, refer to Fig. 2 to draw a half circle on aluminum pan and to punch holes for arms with nail; cut out dress. Place dress on soft surface, then use stylus to emboss designs on back of dress; use hammer to lightly imprint dress with embossing items.

Fig. 2

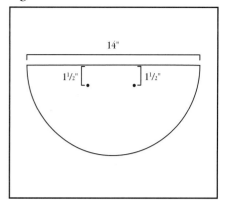

14"

1½"   1½"

4. Spray front of dress with primer, then remaining color of spray paint. Lightly sand to reveal primer and to enhance embossed designs; wipe with tack cloth.

5. For each arm, thread a 3" length of wire through hole in one clothespin piece, then thread both wire ends through hole in dress; spread ends to secure.

6. Wrap dress around body, leaving top of stick for head, and staple at back. Wrap a length of wire around neck several times, twist ends together at front, then curl ends.

7. *Dry Brush*, page 151, wings with white paint; use household cement to attach wings to back of angel.

8. Use pliers to shape one end of a 5" length of hanger wire into a halo. Staple halo to back of head.

9. For hair, apply primer to notebook spiral. Trimming to fit, place wire along top of head and staple to back of head.

TIMELY MOSAIC

Give an old terra-cotta saucer a facelift with pretty pieces of china, tinted grout, and a clock kit. The result is a colorful timepiece with a fanciful alfresco air.

MOSAIC-TILED SAUCER CLOCK

Recycled items: a 7¹/₂" dia. terra-cotta saucer, and broken china and tile pieces

You will also need a drill and ceramic bits, 3" long dowel piece (slightly larger than clock's arbor), silicone adhesive, green acrylic paint, premixed non-sanded tile grout, battery-powered clock module and hands for a 3" to 4" dia. clock face, dark green acrylic spray paint, and a metal washer with hole large enough to accommodate clock's arbor.

1. Drill hole in center of saucer to fit dowel; place dowel in hole.

2. Arranging china and tile pieces as desired, use adhesive to glue pieces to bottom of saucer; carefully remove dowel, then allow adhesive to dry.

3. Add green paint to grout and mix thoroughly to achieve desired color. Follow grout manufacturer's instructions to fill all spaces between china and tile pieces, then clean and polish mosaic surface.

4. Spray paint clock hands dark green and allow to dry.

5. Follow manufacturer's instructions to assemble and attach clock module to clock face. If necessary, use washer as a spacer on back of clock to tighten movement.

Tip: If your clock module does not include a wall hanger, drill a small hole through the top edge of the saucer to attach a length of wire for hanging. Do this before creating mosaic and grouting so you are able to work around the hole and wire.

HEARTFELT KEEPSAKE BOX

*S*pecial treasures and mementos are safely stowed in this stylish chest. Simply dress up an old cigar box with brown paper bags, beverage can cut-outs, and decorative tacks. Lined with felt, this handsome box is just right for any prized possession, from jewelry to collectibles.

STUDDED CIGAR BOX

Recycled items: brown paper bags, cigar box with hinged lid, 12-oz. aluminum beverage can, three glass beads, and scraps of felt

You will also need craft glue, glazing medium, metallic orange acrylic paint, paintbrush, four upholstery tacks, utility scissors, tracing paper, craft crimper (for paper and lightweight metal), decorative thumbtacks, hot glue gun, small nail, wire cutters, and 24-gauge copper jewelry wire.

Use craft glue for all gluing unless otherwise indicated. Allow craft glue and paint to dry after each application.

1. Glue large sections of bags to top and sides of cigar box; trim excess.

2. Reserving a piece of paper for blotting, tear remainder of paper bags into small pieces; glue pieces over box, covering edges.

3. Mix three parts glaze with one part orange paint. Use mixture to paint one section of box, allow to set for a few minutes, then blot with reserved brown paper for texture. Repeat for entire box.

4. Place a tack in bottom corners of box.

5. Cutting through opening in can, cut down can to bottom rim; cut away and discard top and bottom of can. Flatten remaining can piece.

6. Trace heart patterns, page 136, onto tracing paper; cut out. Draw around patterns on printed side of can piece; cut out. Run hearts through crimper.

7. Using thumbtacks and hearts, decorate lid. Cover tack ends with hot glue on inside of lid.

8. For beaded handle, use nail to punch a hole through lid. Thread one bead onto two 6" lengths of wire, fold ends together, then thread through another bead; twist ends close to bead to secure. Thread two of the wire ends through the remaining bead, then down through the hole in the lid. Twist all wires together on inside of box to secure; trim ends.

9. Cut felt pieces to fit inside surfaces of box and glue in place.

*W*ant to create unique shiny-chic jewelry? You "can" do it! Fashioned from aluminum cans and broken Christmas ornaments, this fanciful finery can be engraved with a stylus for a one-of-a-kind look. Brass-colored brads hold this sassy jewelry together.

ALUMINUM CAN JEWELRY

Recycled items: 12-oz. aluminum beverage cans, aluminum foil, and large and small metal toppers from Christmas ornaments

You will also need utility scissors, tracing paper, fine sandpaper, tack cloth, transparent tape, pushpin, gray craft foam, stylus, 1/2"-long brass paper fasteners, washers, 24-gauge gold jewelry wire, wire cutters, jewelry glue, 1/8" dia. hole punch, 1/8" dia. brass eyelets and eyelet tool, small silver braided cord, and pin backs.

HEART NECKLACE

1. Cutting through openings in two cans, cut down sides of cans to bottom rim. Cut away and discard tops and bottoms of cans; flatten remaining can pieces.

2. Trace heart for necklace, large and small leaf, and large and small circle patterns, page 136, onto tracing paper; cut out. Use patterns to make three hearts, four large leaves (two in reverse), two small leaves (one in reverse), five large circles, and four small circles on printed side of can pieces; cut out. Smooth all sharp edges with sandpaper; wipe with tack cloth.

3. Stack hearts with bottom heart silver side down and top two hearts silver side up. Tape pieces together; use pushpin to punch holes through all three hearts as indicated on pattern; untape hearts. Cut a small slit at center of top heart. Working on craft foam on printed side of pieces, use stylus to emboss veins on leaves. Freehand designs on top heart and circles.

4. Thread paper fastener through brass washer, one large circle, then through slit in top heart; bend fastener prongs to back of heart to secure.

5. Restack hearts and use gold wire to "sew" sides and points of hearts together; stuff crushed foil between heart layers to puff heart, then finish sewing hearts together. Twist wire ends together on back of heart to secure; trim ends.

6. Trace four large leaves (two in reverse) and two small leaves (one in reverse) onto craft foam; cut out just inside lines. Glue foam leaves to backs of aluminum leaves. Use hole punch to make holes in all pieces as indicated on patterns.

7. Attach an eyelet to each circle. Use paper fasteners to assemble necklace. Glue remaining circles over holes at ends of leaves.

8. For ties, cut two 9" lengths of braided cord. Tie a large knot in one end of each cord piece; thread cord through holes.

HEART PIN

1. Cutting through opening in can, cut down side of can to bottom rim. Cut away and discard top and bottom of can; flatten remaining can piece.

2. Trace heart for pin pattern, page 136, onto tracing paper; cut out. Use marker to draw around heart three times onto printed side of can piece; cut out. Cut a small slit at center of top heart. Smooth all sharp edges with sandpaper; wipe with tack cloth.

3. Using a large flattened ornament topper in place of the large circle, follow Steps 4 and 5 for the Heart Necklace to complete heart.

4. Glue pin back to heart.

WINGS PIN

1. Cutting through opening in can, cut down side of can to bottom rim. Cut away and discard top and bottom of can; flatten remaining can piece.

2. Trace wings pattern, page 136, onto tracing paper; cut out. Use marker to draw around wings on printed side of can piece; cut out. Smooth all sharp edges with sandpaper; wipe with tack cloth.

3. Place pattern on printed side of wings. Working on craft foam, use stylus to emboss wings.

4. Draw around wings onto craft foam; cut out just inside drawn lines. Glue foam wings to back of aluminum wings. Punch a hole at center of wings.

5. Flatten small ornament topper. Thread paper fastener through brass washer, ornament topper, then through hole in wings; bend fastener prongs to back of wings to secure.

6. Glue pin back to wings.

HEAVENLY HIDEAWAY PENDANT

There's more to this pretty pendant than meets the eye! Constructed from a matchbox, it conceals a secret drawer where you can store anything from a sentimental note to some spare change. Wings are fashioned from an aluminum beverage can, while glass beads and copper wire add a distinctive finishing touch. How divine!

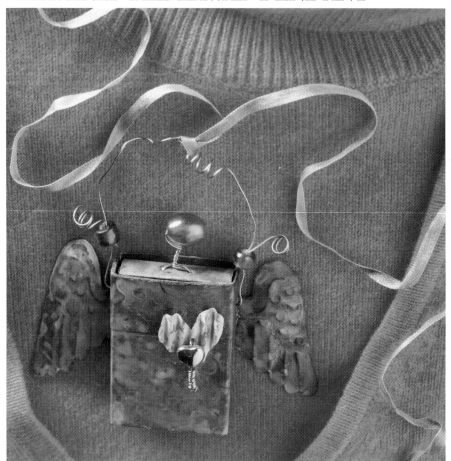

MATCHBOX PENDANT

Recycled items: a small matchbox, 12-oz. aluminum beverage can, natural sponge, toothbrush, and four glass beads

You will also need craft glue; card stock; electrical tape; utility scissors; tracing paper; stylus; craft crimper (for paper and lightweight metal); red metal spray primer; mint green, lime green, pink, and light orange acrylic paint; matte clear acrylic spray sealer; pushpin; wire cutters; 24-gauge copper jewelry wire; large sewing needle; and jewelry glue.

Refer to Painting Techniques, page 151, before beginning project. Allow glue, paint, and sealer to dry after each application.

1. Remove tray from matchbox case. Glue a strip of card stock across bottom and up sides of case, then wrap a piece of electrical tape along top edge.

2. Cutting through opening in can, cut down can to bottom rim; cut away and discard top and bottom of can. Flatten remaining can piece.

3. Trace heart and wings patterns, page 137, onto tracing paper. Use stylus to draw over pattern lines on printed side of can piece; cut out pieces. Run heart through crimper.

4. Center and glue wings onto back of case.

5. Apply primer to case, tray, and heart. Thin green and pink paints with water. *Sponge Paint* case and tray with green paints and heart with pink paint; *Spatter Paint* heart orange. Apply sealer to pieces.

6. Use pushpin to punch a hole in center of heart. Wrap 2" of a 3" length of wire around needle to make tight curls. Place bead on wire, thread wire through hole in heart, then bend wire to back of heart

to secure. Use jewelry glue to attach heart to front of case.

7. Punch a hole, ¹⁄₄" from top, in each side of case. Punch two holes, ¹⁄₄" apart, through one end of tray.

8. Wrap the center of a 12" length of wire several times around a pencil. Thread a bead onto each end of wire. Thread wire ends through holes in case, then back through beads; curl wire ends to secure.

9. Thread remaining bead onto two 3¹⁄₂" lengths of wire. Thread wire ends through holes in tray; twist ends together inside tray to secure. Turn bead to twist wires together.

HANDSOME HINGED BOX

Tuck a tiny treasure in a tasteful trinket box! Egg carton cups make up the basic shape of this exquisite trinket keeper, while gesso and glaze add a faux porcelain finish. Sparkling gold trim completes the ensemble.

EGG-CARTON TRINKET KEEPER

Recycled items: a paper egg carton, newspaper, and a decorative metal keyhole cover

You will also need utility scissors, découpage glue, paintbrushes, gesso, fine sandpaper, tack cloth, clear glaze, acrylic paint, gold paint pen, hot glue gun, $1/2$"-long hinge, and gold trim.

Use découpage glue for all gluing unless otherwise indicated. Allow glue, gesso, glaze, and paint to dry after each application.

1. For each half of keeper, cut two corner cups from egg carton. Glue one cup inside the other; trim tops evenly. Fill indentations by gluing small pieces of egg carton to cups.

2. Tear newspaper into small strips. Cover cups with strips dipped in découpage glue until a smooth surface is achieved.

3. Paint cups with gesso; sand until smooth, then wipe with tack cloth. Paint cups with a thick coat of glaze.

4. Paint cups inside and out (we mixed and swirled our paints). Use paint pen to paint edges of cups and add designs.

5. With cups aligned and being careful not to glue edges together, hot glue hinge to one side of keeper.

6. Apply glaze to keeper. Hot glue trim along edges of keeper and keyhole cover to bottom for stand.

ATTRACTIVE ORGANIZER

*O*ur elegant organizer makes "getting it together" easy. Fashioned from an oversized shoebox and covered with embossed wallpaper, this handy box boasts compartments for each day of the month. Organize bills, coupons, or whatever in an efficient, orderly manner. What a lifesaver!

CARDBOARD BILL ORGANIZER

Recycled items: a large fabric scrap, boot or athletic shoe box (ours measures 12$^1/_2$" x 10$^1/_2$" x 5$^1/_2$"), corrugated cardboard, embossed wallpaper scraps, calendar, and trim or cording scraps

You will also need spray adhesive, craft knife and cutting mat, hot glue gun, toothpick, paintbrushes, cream and assorted colors of acrylic paint, and a stencil brush.

Refer to Measuring Diagram for all project measurements. Use spray adhesive for all gluing unless otherwise indicated. Allow paint to dry after each application.

1. Cut two 3$^1/_2$"w by measurement A and two 3$^1/_2$"w by measurement B strips of fabric. Apply spray adhesive to wrong sides of fabric strips. With $^1/_2$" extending past top edge, smooth strips onto inside of box and over top edges.

2. To make center support, cut a piece of cardboard and fabric, measurement A by 1" shorter than measurement C. To make dividers, cut fifteen pieces of cardboard and fabric, measurement B by measurement C.

3. To cover support and each divider, apply spray adhesive to wrong side of fabric piece. Center and smooth fabric over one long edge of cardboard piece. Center support in box. Hot glue along edges to secure.

4. Using craft knife, cut a narrow vertical slit at center of each divider from bottom to 1" from top. Spacing evenly, slide each divider onto support. Using toothpick, apply a dot of hot glue to each side of dividers at the support to secure.

5. Cut a piece of wallpaper measurement D by measurement C. *Dry Brush*, page 151, wallpaper cream. Use stencil brush to accent the embossed designs with desired colors of paint. Joining ends at back, glue wallpaper around box.

6. For tabs, measure space between two dividers; subtract $^1/_4$". Using determined width, cut five 14" long strips of cardboard. Doubling width, cut five 14" long pieces of fabric. Apply spray adhesive to wrong side of one fabric piece. Center cardboard strip on fabric, then smooth fabric edges over cardboard. Cut strip into 2"-long tabs. Repeat for remaining strips.

7. Make a bend $^3/_4$" from one end on each tab. With top edge of box in bend of tab, hot glue tabs between dividers on each side of box.

8. Cut numbers from calendar to fit on tabs; *Dry Brush* numbers cream. Glue numbers to tabs to represent days of the month. Hot glue trim or cording along top edge of box.

MEASURING DIAGRAM

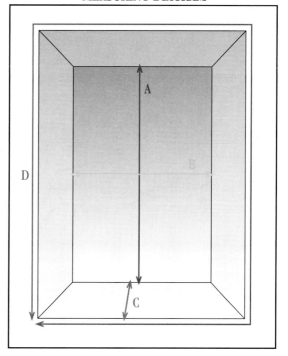

Our sophisticated vase will enrich any home with its safari flair. A coating of shredded paper adds unique texture, and cut-out elephants create an exotic ambience. Lined with a plastic soda bottle, this striking vase is a glamorous way to display cut flowers.

SHREDDED PAPER VASE

Recycled items: shredded paper strips, large round cardboard container (we used a 42-oz. dried oats box), poster board, assorted large beads, and a two-liter plastic beverage bottle

You will also need découpage glue, paintbrushes, metallic copper and metallic taupe acrylic paint, tracing paper, metallic gold rub-on finish, black fine-point permanent marker, 1⅝ yds gold cording, and utility scissors.

Allow glue and paint to dry after each application.

1. Pour a small amount of glue into a bowl; gently mix in a handful of shredded paper until well coated. Apply mixture to container, pressing paper into a compact coating; cover container.

2. Paint container copper.

3. Trace elephant pattern, page 137, onto tracing paper; cut out. Using pattern, cut six elephants from poster board. Paint elephants taupe, then accent with gold finish. Use marker to draw eyes and ears, details on trunk, and outline elephants. Glue elephants around container.

4. Thread one bead onto center of cording, thread ends through remaining beads and knot to secure. Wrap cording around container several times, then knot ends together at back.

5. For liner, cut top from bottle and discard. Place bottom of bottle in container to complete vase.

> *Tip: Achieve a different look by using this technique with a cross-cut or confetti-cut shredder.*

YEAR BOOK FRAME

*T*his scrapbook collage is a real class act. A hardback book cover, dressed up with lined paper and a wooden ruler, makes a sturdy base. Intersperse apple motifs and favorite photos in black cardstock frames. What a great way to "show and tell"!

BOOK COVER FRAME

Recycled items: a book (ours measures 1" x 9¼" x 12¾"), lined notebook paper, wooden ruler, pencils, and silk leaves

You will also need a craft knife, spray adhesive, black and red card stock, thick craft glue, photographs, white gel pen, yellow highlighter, black permanent marker, school-theme scrapbook paper, and tracing paper.

Use craft glue for all gluing unless otherwise indicated.

1. Cut book along inside covers at spine; remove pages.

2. Cut lined paper to fit inside covers of book; use spray adhesive to glue in place. Cut a strip of black card stock to cover inside spine of book; glue in place. Glue ruler to card stock at spine, and glue pencils to ruler.

3. Cut a frame from black card stock to fit each photograph. Use spray adhesive to adhere frames to book and photographs on frames. Use pen to decorate frames.

4. For nameplate, use highlighter to color a strip of lined paper; write child's name with marker. Using spray adhesive, glue lined paper to scrapbook paper; position on book and secure.

5. Trace apple pattern, page 137, onto tracing paper; cut out. Draw around pattern onto red card stock; cut out. Cut small leaves from silk leaves to fit apples; glue apples and leaves to book.

DENIM DESK ORGANIZERS

*L*ooking *for an easy way to get organized? "Hip" denim containers are a perfect fit! Fashioned from worn-out jeans, jackets, jumpers, or skirts, they're just right for outfitting a dorm room or first apartment. Button plackets or jumper straps can be used as decorative edging, and pockets are a fun place to store paper clips or a pair of scissors.*

DENIM-COVERED CONTAINERS

Recycled items: denim clothing and assorted plastic containers with labels removed

You will also need thick craft glue.

Allow glue to dry after each application.

1. For each container, cut a piece from denim large enough to fit around and fold inside and under container.

2. Spread glue onto sides of container and adhere denim piece, folding and gluing denim to inside of container. Clip bottom edges of denim so it lies flat on bottom of container; glue in place. If desired, cut a piece of denim slightly smaller than bottom of container and glue to bottom.

3. Glue a pocket to front of container or a buttoned placket piece along edge of container.

REMINDER MAGNETS

Clever write-on/wipe-off magnets are a great way to keep things running smoothly. By placing clear plastic over notebook paper, you can make them for every member of the family. For fun frames, just cover cardboard from a cereal box with colorful paper or fabric and embellish with buttons or beads. Then turn a candy container into a pen holder for a dry-erase marker that lets you keep track of kids' chores, schedules, to-do items, or even grocery lists.

PLASTIC MESSAGE BOARDS AND MARKER HOLDER

Recycled items: lightweight cardboard (we used a cereal box), decorative paper (we used scrapbooking paper), clear plastic lid from take-out container, heavy-weight cardboard (we used the back of a writing tablet), lined notebook paper, large buttons, wooden clothespins, and a plastic candy container with hinged lid

You will also need spray adhesive, craft knife and cutting mat, craft pinking shears, paintbrush, acrylic paint, black fine-point permanent marker, self-adhesive magnet strips, and decorative-edged craft scissors.

Use craft glue for all gluing unless otherwise indicted. Allow paint and craft glue to dry after each application.

1. For each board, cut a 6¹/₂" x 9" rectangle from lightweight cardboard, decorative paper, clear plastic, heavy-weight cardboard, and notebook paper.

Use spray adhesive to attach decorative paper to lightweight cardboard and notebook paper to heavy-weight cardboard. For frame, cut a 4¹/₄" x 7" opening in lightweight cardboard piece.

2. Glue plastic piece to back of frame, then frame to heavy-weight cardboard piece. Use pinking shears to trim board edges.

3. Glue a button to each corner of board.

4. Disassemble clothespin, paint wooden pieces, then reassemble clothespin. Use marker to write name on clothespin. Attach a piece of magnet along back of clothespin. Clip clothespin to top of board.

5. For pen holder, use craft scissors to cut a piece of decorative paper to fit around candy container; glue in place. Attach a piece of magnet to top of lid; glue button to inside of lid.

EASY ABSTRACT ART

*Y*ou *don't have to be Picasso
to create your own modern art.
Simply cut and arrange quilt
patterns or geometric shapes from
colorful lightweight cardboard. With
a little paint and metallic rub-on
finish, cardboard tubes from pants
hangers form a distinguished frame
for this masterpiece.*

FRAMED QUILT-BLOCK PAPER ART

Recycled items: corrugated cardboard,
brightly-colored twelve-pack beverage
boxes (or other colored paper or
lightweight cardboard products), and
four cardboard pants hanger tubes

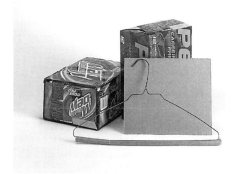

You will also need spray adhesive, black
card stock, quilt block template(s), craft
glue, craft saw and miter box, sandpaper,
tack cloth, paintbrush, black acrylic paint,
metallic silver rub-on finish, and a
soft cloth.

1. For backing, use spray adhesive to
adhere a 12" square of card stock onto
a 12" square of cardboard.

2. Use template(s) to cut shapes from
colored cardboard; arrange and glue
shapes onto backing to create design.

3. Cut strips of colored cardboard to
create a border around design; glue
in place.

4. For frame, use saw and miter box to
cut ends of tubes at 45-degree angles so
they fit together. Sand tube pieces lightly
to remove any sticky residue; wipe with
tack cloth. Paint tubes black; apply silver
finish to tubes, then buff with a soft cloth.
Matching corners, glue tubes along edges
of backing.

*B*righten up your backyard with lively bird lodgings fashioned from colorful plastic bottles. Disposable aluminum cookie sheets or oven liners become rustic roofs, while beaded curlicues add a welcoming touch. Feathered friends will move right in!

PLASTIC BOTTLE BIRDHOUSES

Recycled items: large colorful plastic bottles (we used liquid laundry detergent bottles), small colorful plastic bottles with caps (we used a mustard bottle and a dishwashing liquid bottle), assorted hardware for the perch (we used a pegboard hook and a pipe bracket), screws and nuts, assorted disposable aluminum pans, large craft needle, and plastic beads

You will also need utility scissors, tracing paper, repositionable spray adhesive, awl, brass paper fasteners, wire cutters, craft wire, craft crimper (for lightweight metal and paper).

1. (*Note:* If using a round bottle, cut top from bottle below handle.) For each birdhouse, refer to Fig. 1 as a guide to cut top, sides, and door and punch evenly spaced holes in large bottle.

Fig. 1

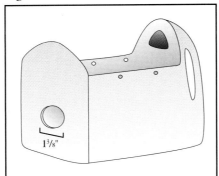

2. For each topper, leaving desired length for petals, cut top section from small bottle; set bottom aside for Step 3. Remove stopper from lid, if needed, and replace cap. Cut sides and ends of petals along bottom edge of topper to create flower shape (some bottles already have a petal-shaped pattern in their design); press topper against a hard surface to bend petals outward.

3. For door flowers, trace desired flower pattern, page 138, onto tracing paper; cut out. Use repositionable spray adhesive to attach flower pattern to bottom of small bottle. Draw around pattern on bottle, then remove pattern and cut out. Aligning door and flower holes, punch through both layers as indicated on pattern; attach flower over door using paper fasteners. Use awl to punch holes for pegboard hanger or pipe bracket; use paper fasteners to attach pipe bracket. Add additional paper fasteners or screws as desired.

4. For each hanger wire, refer to Fig. 2 to attach one end of a 12" length of wire through each hole along top edge of birdhouse; use another length of wire to wrap around hanger wires to secure.

Fig. 2

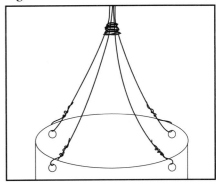

5. For roof on green house, cut a 6$\frac{1}{2}$"w piece of aluminum pan to cover top of birdhouse and hang over edges; run piece through crimper. Leaving a $\frac{1}{2}$" flange, cut a corner edge from aluminum pan the length of crimped roof piece. Overlapping one long edge of roof and flattened corner piece, use wire and needle to "sew" corner edge to front edge of roof; punch a hole in middle of roof.

6. For roof on yellow house, cut two 5$\frac{1}{2}$" x 14" pieces from aluminum pan; run pieces through crimper. Fold short edges of pieces together to form a circle. Gather one long edge of circle to shape top of roof.

7. Thread wires on birdhouse through hole in roof and topper, then bead. Bend three wires down. Wrap bent wires around a pencil and thread a bead onto each wire.

8. Shape end of remaining wire into a hanging loop.

Tip: Mix and match pieces from different bottles to get a variety of bright colors and interesting shapes.

LUMINOUS LANTERN

*G*ive your porch or walkway a comforting glow with a cozy, rustic lantern. Easily made from a coffee can and embellished with simple punched-hole designs, this radiant luminary is reminiscent of primitive folk art. One casts a lovely twinkle, several light up the night!

COFFEE CAN LUMINARY

Recycled items: a 1-lb. coffee can, 12-oz. aluminum beverage cans, lid from a 2-lb. coffee can removed with a safety can opener, and a clothes hanger

You will also need tape, hammer and awl, tin snips, craft crimper (for lightweight metal and paper), wire cutters, silicone adhesive, needle-nose pliers, and a pony bead.

1. Fill coffee can with water to 1" from top and freeze.

2. Enlarge pattern, page 138, by 167%. Tape pattern around can. Using hammer and awl, punch holes in can along pattern lines; remove pattern. Allow ice to melt, then dry can.

3. Use tin snips to cut along holes for front opening.

4. For front edging, cut through opening in aluminum can and down side of can to bottom ridge; cut away top and bottom. Set bottom aside and discard top. Flatten, then cut 1"w strips from aluminum piece; run strips through crimper. Glue crimped strips along edges of opening; allow to dry.

5. Use hammer and awl to punch a hole in center of 2-lb. can lid; punch holes around center hole. Punch two holes on opposite sides of lid to align with handle holes on can.

6. For handle, bend a 10" length of clothes hanger into a U shape. Thread ends through holes in lid and sides of can; bend ends to secure.

7. For rain deflector, make clips ¹/₄" apart along edges of aluminum can bottom; bend tabs outward. Use awl to punch hole in center of rain deflector.

8. Cut a 3" and 4" length from clothes hanger. Using pliers to bend wires, refer to Fig. 1 to assemble and attach rain deflector and hanger.

Fig. 1

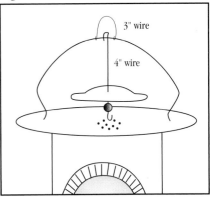

Tip: You can use a design of your own to decorate your candleholder! Cut a piece of paper to fit around can, mark placement holes for handle, then draw your designs. After freezing water in can, use a hammer and awl to punch evenly spaced holes along the lines of your design.

ETHEREAL ANGEL

Add a little bit of heaven to a bare nook or cranny with our guardian angel accent. Paper towel shreds give this angel her wonderfully wispy appearance, and a painted lid or plastic foam circle becomes a tranquil face. Her peaceful presence is a heaven-sent reminder that "godliness and contentment is great gain."

PAPER SHELF SITTER

Recycled items: corrugated cardboard, two 12-oz. aluminum beverage cans, clothes hanger, small metal lid, and a twist-tie

You will also need tracing paper, utility scissors, tape, hot glue gun, black permanent fine-point marker, stylus, wire cutters, spray primer, paper towels, craft glue, white and gold spray paint, paintbrush, and flesh-colored acrylic paint.

Use hot glue for all gluing unless otherwise indicated. Allow paint to dry after each application.

1. Trace body patterns, page 149, onto tracing paper; cut out. Draw around each pattern twice on cardboard; cut out. Referring to Fig. 1, tape pieces together. With tape to the inside, fold body along taped edges; glue edges together to secure. Run a line of glue along each fold and along neck to smooth seam.

Fig. 1

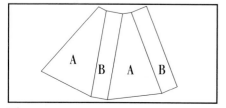

2. Cutting through opening in each can, cut down side of can to bottom rim. Cut away top and bottom; flatten can piece.

3. Trace wings, feathers, and arm patterns, page 150, onto tracing paper; cut out. Use marker to draw around patterns onto can pieces, making two wings, two arms, two small feathers, and two large feathers; cut out. Working on a soft surface, use stylus to emboss wavy lines on wings and feathers. Curl wings and feathers; glue feathers to wings.

4. For head, twist two 4" lengths of hanger wire together. Glue lid to

wire ³/₄" from one end. Shape a halo from twist-tie and secure above lid.

5. Apply primer to body, wings, arms, and head. Glue wings to back of body, arms to sides of body, and wire for neck in top opening of body.

6. Tear paper towels into small pieces and crumple. Use craft glue to cover body with paper towel pieces; allow to dry.

7. Spray paint body white and wings and halo gold. Mist body with gold spray paint.

8. Paint arms and face flesh; use marker to add eyes.

NOSTALGIC NOTIONS COLLAGE

*E*xpress yourself with a personality-portrait — an arrangement of favorite things and meaningful objects. Scraps from craft projects are just right for backdrops and flourishes. Make it sentimental with pressed flowers you've saved or buttons from old clothes. A natural wooden frame highlights the modest beauty of this graceful grouping.

CRAFT SCRAPS COLLAGE

Recycled items: assorted crafting scraps (we used wrapping paper, card stock, gift sacks, colored corrugated craft cardboard, buttons, jewelry pieces, beads, dried florals, and napkins)

You will also need a frame with backing and craft glue.

1. Remove backing from frame.

2. For background, arrange and glue wrapping paper and card stock on backing.

3. Arrange remaining scraps on background and glue in place.

4. Secure collage in frame.

FUNNY FACE MOBILE

PLASTIC LID FACES MOBILE

A kid-friendly mobile is just the thing to cultivate young imaginations. Little ones help create these funny faces by gluing pom-poms, scraps of trim, and wiggly eyes to fabric-lined plastic lids. Finish by dangling the colorful faces from crisscrossed cardboard tubes. This wacky mobile is a great family project for children ages 5 and up.

Recycled items: colored plastic lids, fabric and batting scraps, lightweight cardboard, assorted craft supplies (we used ribbon and trim scraps, pom-poms, self-adhesive wiggle eyes, and chenille stems), and three cardboard pants hanger tubes

You will also need white poster board, craft glue, 1/16" dia. hole punch, wire cutters, plastic-coated colored craft wire, opaque paint pens, sandpaper, tack cloth, paintbrush, yellow acrylic paint, low-temperature glue gun, and large pom-poms.

Note: This project is fun for kids five years and older to make with adult supervision. It is not intended for use in cribs and contains small parts that could cause choking hazards for small children.

Use craft glue for all gluing unless otherwise indicated. Allow craft glue and paint to dry after each application.

1. For each face, draw around lid on fabric, batting, lightweight cardboard, and poster board. Cut out fabric circle 5/8" outside drawn line; cut out remaining circles just inside drawn lines. Clip edges of fabric piece to drawn line.

2. Center batting circle, then cardboard circle, on wrong side of fabric circle. Wrap edges of fabric to back of cardboard and glue in place. Glue poster board to back of cardboard.

3. For hanger, punch a hole through rim of lid. Thread wire through hole. Bend wire end to catch on inside of lid; glue to secure. With fabric side out, glue covered circle in lid; glue trim along fabric edge.

4. With hanger at top, create face and hair on front of lid using paint pens and craft supplies.

5. For mobile frame, sand cardboard tubes lightly to remove any sticky residue; wipe with tack cloth. Paint tubes yellow. Cross two tubes at center; use hot glue to hold tubes in place while wrapping wire tightly around intersection to secure.

6. Attach another piece of wire to center of crossed tubes, then wrap wire around center of third tube for next level; twist to secure, leaving enough wire at top for hanger. Glue large pom-poms to ends of tubes.

7. Wrap hangers on faces around frame, adjusting until the mobile hangs level; curl wire ends around a pencil.

Tip: Hang tube frame before attaching faces, so both hands are free to help balance mobile.

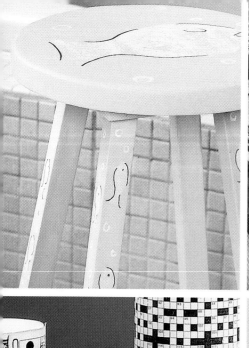

second chances

A fresh coat of paint and a little "trash" can give scratched or scuffed furniture, accessories, and more a long and useful life. Add sparkle and shine to photo frames with beverage can trimmings. Transform an old ottoman into a teaching tool for children. Craft a clever bathroom accessory from a castoff stool. You'll love how these magical makeovers give ragtag furnishings a second chance.

Turn a tattered ottoman into a toddler's learning center. Brightly colored fabrics capture a youngster's attention, while buttons, buckles, zippers, and shoelaces tutor tots in the basics of dressing themselves. You'll love this helpful hands-on teaching tool!

OTTOMAN LEARNING CENTER

Recycled items: a square ottoman, four large buttons, two pieces of clothing with zippers, lace-up canvas tennis shoe, shoestring, child-size overalls, belts, and belt loops from pants

You will also need four solid fabrics and one print fabric, fabric glue, hot glue gun, and felt.

Match right sides and raw edges and use a ¹/₂" seam allowance for all sewing. Use fabric glue for all gluing unless otherwise indicated.

1. Measure width and height of sides and top of ottoman. Adding 1" to width and 1¹/₂" to height, cut a piece of solid fabric for each side panel. Cut a piece of print fabric ¹/₂" larger on all sides than top of ottoman.

2. For each button flap on top panel, cut two same-size triangles from solid fabric. Sew triangles together along point, clip point, then turn and press. Make a buttonhole at point. Center a flap on each edge of top fabric piece and baste in place. Sew button to top fabric piece, then button flap.

3. For zipper panel, remove zippers from clothing; turn edges under and sew to solid fabric panel.

4. For lacing panel, cut top from shoe. Using a wide zigzag stitch and leaving top around tongue unattached, sew shoe piece to solid fabric panel. Lace shoestring through eyelets.

5. For overall panel, cut bib from overalls; glue bib to solid fabric panel. Leaving straps long enough to buckle, cut straps from overalls and sew to panel.

6. For belt panel, cut belts same width as fabric panel; baste cut ends to edges of panel. Glue belt loops over belts.

7. Center and sew one panel to each edge of top piece, then sew side pieces together along edges. Hem bottom edge ¹/₄".

8. Place cover over ottoman. Gathering as necessary, hot glue bottom edge of cover to bottom of ottoman.

9. Glue a square of felt over bottom of ottoman.

HINGED TOWEL BAR

*W*ith just a little paint, you can create a trendy towel holder from a salvaged table leg. Hinged to the wall, this handy towel bar folds away when not in use, so it's ideal for confined spaces. A wooden finial and a painted floral pattern add an air of sophistication.

TABLE LEG TOWEL HOLDER

Recycled items: a wooden table leg

You will also need primer; hinge and hardware; wood glue; finial; paintbrushes; green, red, and gold acrylic paint; tracing paper; stylus; transfer paper; gold fine-point paint pen; and matte clear acrylic sealer.

Allow primer, paint, and sealer to dry after each application.

1. Refer to Fig. 1 to attach hinge to leg. Apply primer, then paint hinge to match wall.

Fig. 1

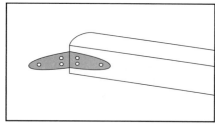

2. Glue finial to end of leg. Apply primer to towel holder; paint large sections green, small sections red, and seams gold.

3. Trace flower pattern, page 139, onto tracing paper. Use stylus and transfer paper to transfer pattern onto towel holder as desired; paint over pattern lines with red paint and accent with paint pen.

4. Use paint pen to draw vines with leaves connecting flowers.

5. Apply sealer to towel holder.

SPLISH-SPLASH STOOL

*S*plish! Splash! Dress up your bath with a fun fish stool. Shades of blue and green refresh a worn wooden stool and conjure the calming aura of the sea. Add a fishy family with stamps made from foam packing material and cardboard scraps. Simply "splashing"!

PAINTED STOOL

Recycled items: a wooden stool, thick foam packing sheet, and corrugated cardboard

You will also need spray primer, paintbrushes, assorted colors of acrylic paint, tracing paper, craft glue, permanent marker, and matte clear acrylic spray sealer.

Allow primer, paint, and glue to dry after each application.

1. Apply primer to stool, then paint desired color.

2. For fish stamps, trace patterns, page 140, onto tracing paper; cut out. Draw around patterns onto foam; cut out. Cut cardboard pieces slightly larger than fish. Glue two cardboard pieces together for each stamp; glue stamp to cardboard.

3. Paint stamp desired color; stamp large fish on seat of stool. Repeat to stamp small fish on legs; use marker to outline fish and add eyes. Paint bubbles on stool.

4. Apply sealer to stool.

BREAKFAST-IN-BED TRAY

*R*ise and shine! You'll love waking up to breakfast served on this happy-go-lucky bed table. Matching picture frames make a sturdy tray, and a flowered tablecloth is a cheerful backdrop. Not a morning person? This versatile tray is also great for reading or writing in bed!

FRAMED BED TRAY

Recycled items: two large matching frames with hardboard backing (ours measure 20$\frac{1}{2}$" x 24$\frac{1}{2}$"), plastic packing straps (we used yellow straps), $\frac{1}{2}$-gal. yellow plastic jug, four buttons, two cabinet handles with hardware, and a vinyl tablecloth

You will also need a saw, sandpaper, tack cloth, four 2" long corner brackets and two 3" long corner brackets with hardware, white spray primer, white spray paint, household adhesive, craft glue, decorative trim, decorative-edged craft scissors, paintbrush, and yellow acrylic paint.

Use household adhesive for all gluing unless otherwise indicated. Allow primer, paint, household adhesive, and craft glue to dry after each application.

1. For tray legs, cut one frame in half at center of each long end. Cut legs to desired height; sand and wipe with tack cloth. Referring to Fig. 1 and using corner brackets, attach legs to bottom of second frame.

Fig. 1

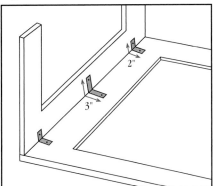

2. Apply primer to tray, then paint tray frame white.

3. For border, glue lengths of packing strap around frame, then use craft glue to glue lengths of trim along outer edges of packing straps.

4. Using craft scissors, cut four circles from jug and glue them over corners of border. Glue buttons to circles.

5. Apply primer to handles, then paint yellow. Attach handles to tray frame.

6. For tray top, cut a piece from tablecloth that is 2" larger on all sides than one frame backing. Center backing on wrong side of tablecloth piece, fold and glue tablecloth edges to back of backing. Glue covered backing to remaining backing and secure in frame.

CACTUS FLOWER PICNIC CADDY

*B*ring home a little piece of the Southwest with this rustic kitchen caddy. A wooden soda crate is duded up with horseshoe handles, bottle cap flowers, and a patch of cacti for a "Wild West" flair. Pretty and practical, this primitive tray makes transporting items from kitchen to patio hassle-free.

CAP-STUDDED SERVING CRATE

Recycled items: a wooden soda crate, clear plastic take-out tray, natural sponge, metal bottle caps, and two horseshoes

You will also need a saw; paintbrushes; red, light green, green, and orange acrylic paint; craft knife and cutting mat; black, green, and red paint pens; hammer and awl; #4 carpet tacks; screws and screwdriver; and matte clear acrylic spray sealer.

Allow paint and sealer to dry after each application.

1. Use saw to cut away dividers in crate to enlarge holders. Paint inside of crate red; paint outside wooden areas light green.

2. Following *Stenciling*, page 152, use cactus and squares pattern, page 140, to make a stencil from take-out tray. Spacing evenly, stencil green cacti and orange squares on sides of crate.

3. Use black paint pen to draw dashed lines around squares and to outline and draw spines on cacti. Use green paint pen to dot center of each square.

4. Use hammer to flatten bottle caps. For each flower, use hammer and awl to punch a hole at center of cap. Use green paint pen to paint center of flower.

5. Use tacks to attach flowers to top of each cactus. Use red paint pen to paint tacks.

6. For handles, paint horseshoes red; use screws to attach to ends of crate.

7. Apply sealer to crate.

FLASHY PHOTO FRAMES

*P*icture this: whimsical "can-did" photo frames in no time flat! Make shabby photo frames shimmer with metallic paint and aluminum can cut-outs such as stars, curlicues, or other simple shapes. Add a favorite picture for a precious keepsake or a fanciful gift.

CAN EMBELLISHED FRAMES

Recycled items: wooden frames, 12-oz. aluminum beverage cans, and a natural sponge

You will also need paintbrushes; blue, metallic gold, and matte gold acrylic paint; utility scissors; tracing paper; hammer and awl; #2 carpet tacks; gold paint pen; and matte clear acrylic spray sealer.

Refer to Painting Techniques, page 151, before beginning projects. Allow paint and sealer to dry after each application.

SMALL FRAME

1. Paint frame blue.

2. Cutting through opening in can, cut down can to bottom rim; cut away and discard top and bottom of can. Flatten remaining can piece.

3. Trace star pattern, page 140, onto tracing paper; cut out. Draw around pattern onto can piece; cut out (we cut out twenty stars).

4. Use hammer and awl to punch a hole through center of each star; use tacks to attach stars to frame.

5. Using paint pen, paint tops of tacks and outline stars; paint dots between stars.

6. Apply two coats of sealer to frame.

LARGE FRAME

1. Paint frame metallic gold, then *Sponge Paint* using matte gold paint.

2. Cutting through opening in can, cut down can to bottom rim; cut away and discard top and bottom of can. Flatten remaining can piece.

3. Trace spiral patterns, page 140, onto tracing paper; cut out. Draw around patterns onto can piece; cut out (we cut out ten spirals).

4. Use hammer and awl to punch holes through spirals in several places; use tacks to attach spirals to frame.

5. Using paint pen, paint tops of tacks.

6. Apply two coats of sealer to frame.

FAUX-FINISH FLOOR LAMP

*D*on't throw away that rusty old floor lamp — transform it into an eye-catching accent with a few simple painting techniques and a chic fabric-covered lampshade! A textured basecoat covers previous problem areas. For a pearly stained-glass glow, illuminate selected sections with a special combination of paints. Gorgeous!

FAUX-FINISHED BRASS FLOOR LAMP AND LAMPSHADE COVER

Recycled items: a brass floor lamp, natural sponge, and a lampshade

You will also need spray primer; masking tape; paintbrushes; green, light green, yellow, rusty brown, light orange, and white acrylic paint; liquid polyurethane coating; matte clear acrylic sealer; brush-on gloss clear acrylic sealer; fabric; string; hot glue gun; moss fringe; and gimp.

LAMP

Refer to Painting Techniques, page 151, before beginning project. More than one coat of paint may be necessary for desired coverage. Allow paint and sealer to dry after each application.

1. Apply primer to lamp; mask areas that will be painted with the stained glass technique. Paint remainder of lamp green, then *Sponge Paint* with a mixture of one part light green paint and two parts polyurethane. Apply matte sealer to green areas of lamp. Remove tape.

2. Follow Steps 3 – 6 to paint all stained glass areas.

3. Paint areas yellow, then *Sponge Paint* lightly with a mixture of one part water and three parts rusty brown paint.

4. Using mixtures of one part paint and three parts polyurethane, paint areas with uneven strokes of green, light green, and light orange paint.

5. Paint areas with a mixture of one part white paint and three parts polyurethane. Lightly streak with a mixture of one part light orange paint and three parts polyurethane.

6. Apply gloss sealer.

LAMPSHADE COVER

Match right sides and raw edges and use a ¹/₂" seam allowance for all sewing.

1. Measure height of lampshade; add 6". Measure around bottom edge of shade; add 1". Cut a piece of fabric determined measurements. Sew short edges of fabric piece together; turn right side out and press seam open.

2. For bottom casing, press raw edge of fabric ¹/₈" to wrong side; press ⁵/₈" to wrong side again. Leaving a ¹/₂" opening, sew along casing edge (Fig. 1); thread string through casing. Repeat for top casing.

Fig. 1

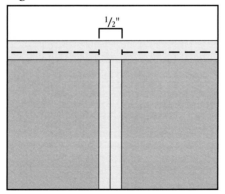

3. Place cover on shade.

4. Referring to Fig. 2 for bottom of shade, pull both ends of string to tighten cover around bottom of shade. Knot and trim string ends, then *Whipstitch, page 153,* along bottom of shade to secure in place.

Fig. 2

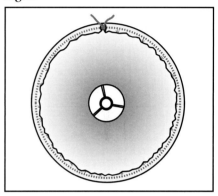

5. For top of shade, pull both ends of string to gather cover against edge of shade; knot and trim string ends. Twist top edge of cover around shade and pin in place. *Whipstitch* along top of shade to secure in place.

6. Glue a length of fringe along top edge of shade, then glue gimp over edge of fringe.

NIFTY BELTED NAPKINS

*L*iven up the dinner table with playful napkin sets. These "recycled" creations are full of fun, and they're a cinch to make from cast-off belts. Pair with frayed fabric squares for colorful coordinates ... a perfect fit for a casual meal with friends!

BELT NAPKIN RINGS WITH NAPKINS

Recycled items: leather belts and large fabric scraps

You will also need utility scissors, household adhesive, and clothespins.

NAPKIN RINGS
1. For each napkin ring, cut an 8" piece from the tab end of a belt. Forming a ring, overlap 2" of tab end and glue; secure with clothespin until dry.

2. Remove keeper loop from buckle end of belt; glue loop around ring where tab end overlaps. Secure with clothespins until dry.

NAPKINS
1. For each napkin, cut a 22" square from fabric scrap; fray edges of fabric.

2. Place napkin in napkin ring.

TEXTURED SPHERES

You'll have a ball garnishing your home with these tasteful textured spheres. Simply made from plastic balls and recycled materials like mesh produce bags, bubble wrap, or egg carton pulp, our crackled creations add an earthy element to your décor.

TEXTURED PLASTIC BALLS

Recycled items: a mesh produce bag, soft plastic balls (ours measure 3³/₅" dia.), tissue paper, bubble wrap, and a paper egg carton

You will also need household adhesive; thick craft glue; paintbrushes; gold, brown, green, and tan acrylic paint; two buckets; rubber gloves; and a blender.

Allow glue and paint to dry after each application.

MESH-COVERED BALL

1. Use household adhesive to glue a piece of mesh bag to ball, covering completely. Using craft glue, cover ball with tissue paper.

2. Paint ball gold, then *Dry Brush,* page 151, brown.

BUBBLE WRAP-COVERED BALL

1. Use household adhesive to glue bubble wrap to ball, covering completely. Using craft glue, cover ball with tissue paper.

2. Paint ball green, then *Dry Brush,* page 151, brown.

PAPIER-MÂCHÉ-COVERED BALL

1. Tear egg carton into ¹/₂" pieces; place in bucket. Fill bucket with hot water and soak pieces for at least an hour.

2. Wearing rubber gloves, squeeze excess water from a small handful of pre-soaked paper pieces and place in blender; cover with water until blender is half full.

Blend at low speed for fifteen seconds, increasing speed to medium, then high, at fifteen-second intervals; decrease speed in the same manner. When pulp is no longer lumpy, pour into second bucket. Repeat the blending process until all pieces have been processed.

3. Scoop pulp from bucket and add a small amount of craft glue to pulp. Squeeze excess water from mixture. Cover ball completely with mixture and allow to dry.

4. Paint ball tan, then *Dry Brush,* page 151, brown.

93

PLAYFUL PILLARS

*I*f you're game for a clever conversation piece, you'll love our witty creations. Simply dress up a center-burning candle with cards, checkers, puzzle pieces, marbles, even a crossword puzzle! These humorous candles are just right for setting a leisurely mood.

GAME PIECE-COVERED CANDLES

Recycled items: playing cards, mesh marble bag, marbles, jigsaw puzzle pieces, crossword puzzle, window screen, and checkers

You will also need ¹/₂"-long straight pins, center-burning pillar candles, hot glue gun, clear nylon thread and needle (optional), découpage glue, wire cutters, and pliers.

Caution: Use only center-burning candles. Use hot glue for all gluing unless otherwise indicated.

CARD CANDLE
1. Pinning cards in each corner, cover candle with cards turned lengthwise and face-side down.

2. Glue a second layer of cards, face-side up, on top of first layer.

MARBLE AND PUZZLE PIECE CANDLES
1. Cover outside of each candle with mesh bag, making sure bag fits snugly around candle. If necessary, cut bag to fit, then sew together with clear thread.

2. Glue marbles or jigsaw puzzle pieces to mesh. If necessary, insert pins into candle below game pieces for support.

CROSSWORD PUZZLE CANDLE
1. Cut out crossword puzzle; reduce or enlarge image to fit around candle.

2. Using découpage glue, follow manufacturer's instructions to adhere and seal puzzle around candle.

CHECKERS CANDLE
1. Cut a piece from screen to fit candle. Using pliers, bend edges of screen to inside. Wrap screen around candle; pin in place.

2. Glue checkers to screen.

"NOTE-WORTHY" MOSAIC TABLE

This musical mosaic makes a "notable" addition to any room. Black and white paint turns a time-scarred table into a tasteful accent, while a variety of buttons work in perfect harmony to form an enchanting "two-tone" design. Now that's something to sing about!

BUTTON MOSAIC TABLE

Recycled items: a small round wooden table and black and white buttons

You will also need white spray primer, paintbrushes, white and black acrylic paint, craft glue, pre-mixed white tile grout, grout sealer, and matte clear acrylic spray sealer.

Allow primer, paint, glue, grout, and sealer to dry after each application.

1. Apply primer then white paint to table; accent spindle with black paint.

2. Arrange black buttons into musical notes on tabletop and glue to secure. Glue white buttons to remainder of tabletop and along rim.

3. Add one drop of black paint to grout and mix thoroughly; apply mixture to tabletop according to manufacturer's instructions.

4. Apply grout sealer to tabletop and matte sealer to painted areas.

Beth

celebrations

There's no doubt about it — "discards" can help make holidays and special occasions even more festive! Set the mood with a Christmas topiary made from recycled odds and ends. Craft tiny gift boxes from old greeting cards. Round up leftover wrapping paper, useless light bulbs, empty soap containers, and cast-off cans, and transform them into fun and festive adornments. No matter what the occasion, these projects will inspire you to celebrate in style.

"BE MINE" VALENTINE BOX

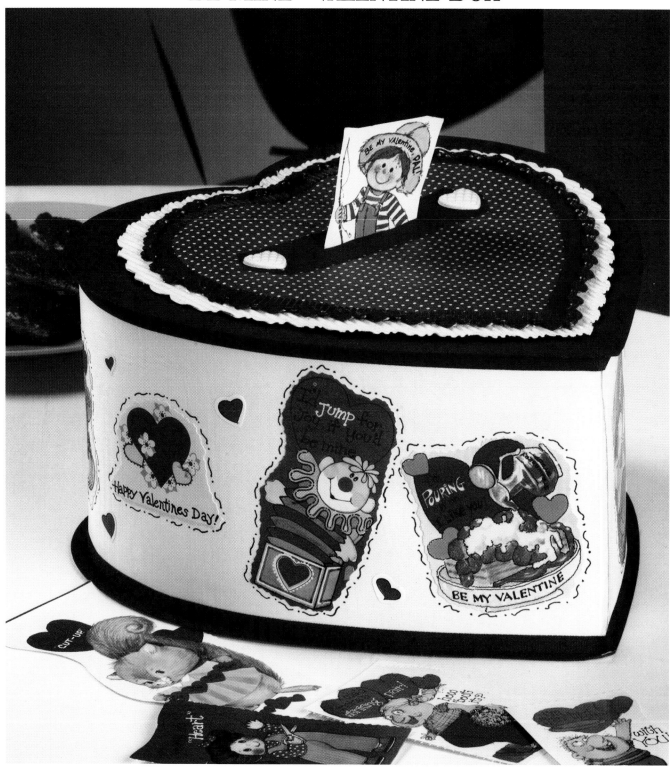

*O*ur cute container is just right for collecting cards during a Valentine's Day party at school. Two heart-shaped candy boxes give the container its sweet shape, while cut-out valentines and bits of ribbon add a heartfelt touch. Kids will love to help with the painting and gluing, so spend some time creating fond memories with a special child!

CANDY BOX VALENTINE CONTAINER

Recycled items: small and large heart-shaped candy boxes (ours measure $6^5/8$"w and 9"w across widest part of hearts), and valentines

You will also need decorative paper, white corrugated cardboard, utility scissors, craft knife and cutting mat, decorative-edge craft scissors, paintbrush, red acrylic paint, poster board, hot glue gun, assorted ribbon (ours measures $1/4$"w, $3/8$"w, and $5/8$"w), craft glue, valentine stickers, black permanent fine-point marker, decorative trim, and two heart-shaped buttons with shanks removed.

Use craft glue for all gluing unless otherwise indicated. Allow paint and craft glue to dry after each application.

1. Trace around inside lip of small heart box lid onto decorative paper, cardboard, and center top of large heart box; cut out heart shapes from paper and top of box. Use craft scissors to cut out cardboard shape $1/2$" outside drawn lines.

2. Paint top of large box lid and entire bottom of large box red.

3. To make sides of container, refer to Fig. 1 and measure around one side of large heart box lip from top center of heart to bottom of heart, then cut a 5"w strip of poster board the determined measurement (A). Adding 1" to the same measurement, cut another piece of poster board (B). Fold one end of B strip $1/2$" to shiny side and the other end $1/2$" to dull side.

Fig. 1

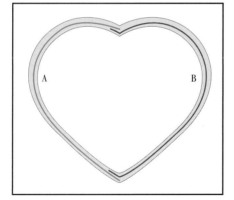

4. With dull side facing out and folded ends of B strip fitting in top center and around bottom point of heart lip, hot glue B strip, then A strip around lip of box bottom.

5. Hot glue lip of large box lid into container.

6. Measure around container; cut two lengths of ribbon the determined measurement. Glue ribbon lengths along top and bottom edges of container sides. Use craft scissors to trim edges of valentines. Glue valentines to sides of container, then apply stickers. Use marker to draw decorative borders around valentines.

7. For lid, glue paper heart to center of cardboard heart; glue cardboard heart to top of small heart lid. Glue $3/8$"w ribbon over edges of paper heart; glue trim along ribbon edges. Use craft knife to cut a slot across center of lid. Cut two lengths of $5/8$"w ribbon with angled ends and glue along edges of slot; glue buttons to ribbon at each end of slot. Place lid on container.

SENTIMENTAL HEARTS

*I*f you think empty soda cans are useless, these sentimental pins will give you a change of heart. Simply cut pieces of cast-off cans into delicate heart shapes, then enhance the charming pins with tiny wire curlicues. What a wonderful way to add a touch of warmth to your winter wardrobe!

ALUMINUM CAN PINS

Recycled items: a 12-oz. aluminum beverage can

You will also need utility scissors, blue permanent fine-point marker, rusted metal heart cutouts, hammer, tool to make designs in metal (we used an awl, the square end of a file, and a flathead screwdriver), sandpaper, tack cloth, soft cloth, gold and red acrylic paint, paintbrush, silver paint pen, 20-gauge craft wire, wire cutters, assorted glass beads, household cement, and pin backs.

Note: When embossing metal, place hearts on a scrap of craft foam or wood to protect work surface.

1. For each pin, cut through opening in can down to bottom rim; cut away and discard top and bottom of can. Flatten can piece.

2. Use marker to draw around rusted heart on printed side of can piece. Cutting ¹/₂" outside drawn lines, cut desired edging for pin (we cut one heart with a smooth edge and one with a scalloped edge). Working on silver side of can, lightly tap hammer on tool to emboss designs along edges of hearts; lightly sand edges of can heart, then wipe with tack cloth.

3. Use soft cloth to rub gold paint over can heart; wipe off excess paint and allow to dry. If desired, outline embossed designs with marker. Paint edges of rusted heart red, then accent with paint pen.

4. Place rusted heart on can heart; use hammer and awl or a small nail to punch a hole through both hearts near the top; sand any sharp edges on back of can heart.

5. Bend an 8" length of wire in half; insert bend through holes in hearts and flatten against back of can heart. Twist wire ends around a small paintbrush handle to create spirals; add beads and curl wire ends to secure.

6. Glue pin back to hearts; allow to dry.

"EGGS-TRAORDINARY" EASTER BASKET

*G*et things hopping with a
vibrantly colored Easter basket
made from recycled household items.
Covered with decorative napkins,
a plastic jug has plenty of room for
candy or coordinating eggs. Foam
embellishments and purchased
notions make this whimsical
project bloom.

DÉCOUPAGED PLASTIC BASKET

Recycled items: large plastic container
(we used a large liquid soap refill
container), craft foam scraps, rubber
band, 18" piece of ³/₄" dia. clear rubber
tubing, tissue paper, and Easter grass
and ornaments

You will also need a utility knife,
découpage glue, 2-ply decorative napkins,
hot glue gun, three 3-yd lengths of
coordinating ¹/₂"w ribbons, and craft wire.

Allow glue to dry after each application.

1. For basket, use utility knife to cut away
top of container.

2. Follow *Découpage*, page 152, to
cover basket with top plies of napkins.
Cut selected motifs from top plies of
additional napkins and découpage
over matching motifs on basket.

3. To embellish basket, cut shapes from
craft foam to accent napkin designs, then
arrange and hot glue to basket.

4. Use utility knife to cut two ¹/₂"w
horizontal slits 2" from top on opposite
sides of basket.

5. Cut each ribbon into three 1-yd
lengths. Separate ribbon into three groups
with one of each color. Knot one end of
each group together; loosely braid, and
secure other end with rubber band.

6. For handle, wrap one end of wire
around loose end of braid; thread wire
from inside, through slit in basket, pulling
braid through and catching knot on
inside. Thread wire and braid through
tubing. On opposite side of basket, thread
wire from outside to inside and pull braid
through slit. Remove wire; knot braid on
inside and trim excess.

7. Starting underneath one side of handle,
hot glue another braid around top edge
of one side of basket; cross over opposite
handle, and glue braid along other side
of basket. Cross over handle at starting
point; tuck ends under, and glue in place.

8. Hot glue remaining braid around
bottom of basket; overlapping braid
and trimming excess, tuck end under
and glue in place.

9. Line basket with tissue paper, then fill
with Easter grass. Attach ornaments to
basket handle.

ENCHANTING SPRING TREE

*A*s spring approaches, this dainty accent is a lovely way to freshen up your décor. Just fashion the tree with tiers of aluminum cut from beverage cans and anchor them to a broom-handle trunk. Corrugated kraft paper makes a breezy cover for the flowerpot base, and pastel candies add a sweet touch to this perfectly pretty tree.

ALUMINUM CAN TREE

Recycled items: a 6" dia. disposable plastic flowerpot, 18" length cut from broom handle, and fifteen 12-oz. aluminum beverage cans

You will also need corrugated kraft paper; craft glue; decorative-edge craft scissors; white poster board; white spray primer; paintbrushes; light orange and pink acrylic paint; craft sponge; clear acrylic sealer; orange and green spray paint; hammer; 1½"-long thin nail with a head; plaster of paris; utility scissors; tracing paper; ⅛" dia. hole punch; orange, pink, green, and white dimensional paint; wire cutters; 26-gauge craft wire; hot glue gun; green thread; plastic plate; aluminum foil; and Easter candies.

Use craft glue for all gluing unless otherwise indicated. Allow primer, paint, and craft glue to dry after each application.

1. For container, cut irregular shapes from corrugated paper to cover lower part of pot. Fitting shapes together at different angles and trimming as needed, glue in place. Use craft scissors to cut a strip ⅜"w by circumference of pot bottom. Glue strip along bottom edge of pot.

2. Measure circumference of top edge of pot; cut a piece of poster board 1½"w by the determined measurement. With edge of strip extending ½" above rim of pot, glue in place. Cut one strip each of poster board and kraft paper 2"w by circumference of rim plus ¼". Matching long edges, glue strips together. Use craft scissors to trim one long edge. With decorative edge even with bottom edge of poster board rim, glue strip in place.

3. Apply primer, then light orange paint to container. Using sponge, lightly paint only the top ridges of kraft paper pink. Apply two coats of sealer.

4. For trunk, apply primer, then orange spray paint to broom handle. Hammer nail into top center of broom handle, leaving the nail extending 1" above handle. Follow manufacturer's instructions to mix plaster. Pour plaster into container to within 1" from top and let set briefly; insert 3" of trunk into plaster. Allow plaster to harden completely.

5. For tree boughs, cut through openings and down sides of cans to bottom rims. Cut away and discard tops and bottoms of cans; flatten remaining pieces.

6. Trace tree patterns, page 141, onto tracing paper; cut out. Use patterns to draw one treetop, seven large, four medium, and five small tree tiers on can pieces; cut out. Punch holes in treetop and tiers where indicated. Make ¼" cuts at ¼" intervals along top edge of each tier as indicated on pattern.

7. Apply primer, then two coats of green spray paint to the front and back of treetop and tiers. Use dimensional paint to draw flowers, leaves, and border stripes along bottom edges.

8. To attach tiers to trunk, weave a 6" length of wire through holes in top edge of each tier. Bend top edges up to form tabs. Starting 7" from plaster base with largest tier and working upward, hot glue tabs to trunk. Twist wire ends together tightly; trim excess wire. For treetop, overlap and lace up edges with thread to form cone shape, leaving a small opening in the top. Pull thread tight and knot; set treetop on nail at top of trunk. To secure, make a "tree topper" with pink dimensional paint (paint should go on nail head and over top point of cone).

9. Cover plaster base with plate and aluminum foil cut to fit; fill with Easter candies.

ALL-AMERICAN ART

Land of the Free

Home of the Brave

Soar to new heights with our bold patriotic wall hanging. Painted on a leftover scrap of vinyl flooring, this flag-waving design features Old Glory and a valiant eagle. What a fitting tribute to the courageous American spirit!

PAINTED VINYL WALL HANGING

Recycled items: a 2' x 3' piece of vinyl floor covering, two yardsticks, clear plastic take-out container lid, and two wood strips approximately 2" x 21½"

You will also need white primer; paintbrushes; gold, blue, red, and black acrylic paint; black permanent fine-point marker; 2"h letter stencils; clear acrylic sealer; household adhesive; and two picture hangers

Allow primer, paint, sealer, and adhesive to dry after each application. More than one coat of paint may be necessary for desired coverage.

1. Apply two to three coats of primer to wrong side of vinyl.

2. Use a yardstick and pencil to lightly draw a 2½"w border along edges of vinyl. Draw a triangle for field of blue and wavy stripes within border.

3. Paint border gold.

4. Enlarge eagle pattern, page 142, 210%; cut out. Use marker to draw over lines of star pattern, page 142, onto plastic lid; cut out. Lightly draw around star pattern inside the field as many times as desired. Arrange, then lightly draw around eagle pattern over stripes. Use stencils to form words along the top and bottom borders.

5. Paint words and field around stars blue. Painting around eagle, paint alternating stripes red. Paint eagle black.

6. Apply two to three coats of sealer to wall hanging.

7. Glue yardsticks and wood strips along back edges of vinyl. Attach picture hangers to back of top yardstick.

ALL-STAR LIBERTY WREATH

*T*his radiant wreath is a spectacular way to salute the land that you love. A foam circle découpaged with torn newspaper serves as the base for our eye-catching accent, and stars cut from foam plates add extra dazzle. Display it in honor of Independence Day or to show your patriotism.

PLASTIC FOAM WREATH

Recycled items: newspaper and plastic foam plates

You will also need a 16" dia. plastic foam wreath; découpage glue; spray primer; paintbrushes; silver, red, white, and blue acrylic paint; gold metallic rub-on finish; tracing paper; utility scissors; red, white, and blue dimensional paint; hot glue gun; $1/16$" dia. hole punch; and small gold cording.

Use hot glue for all gluing unless otherwise indicated. Allow découpage glue, primer, and paint to dry after each application.

1. Tear newspaper into small strips. Cover wreath with newspaper strips dipped in découpage glue until a smooth surface is achieved.

2. Apply primer, then two coats of silver paint to wreath. Apply finish to wreath; wipe away excess.

3. Trace star patterns, page 143, onto tracing paper; cut out. Use patterns to cut enough assorted sizes of stars from plates to overlap and cover wreath. Apply primer, then paint each star red, white, or blue. Use finger to apply streaks of finish across stars. Use a coordinating color of dimensional paint to outline each star.

4. Setting aside three stars (one of each color and size) to hang in center of wreath, glue remaining stars to wreath.

5. To hang remaining stars, punch a hole in one point of each star. Thread one end of a length of cording through hole and knot at front of star. Glue remaining ends of cording to back of wreath.

"EERIE-SISTIBLE" HALLOWEEN LAMP

Light up the night with our bewitching Halloween lamp. A large glass jar encases a ghostly scene, and a kraft-paper lampshade adorned with cut motifs casts an eerie glow. Try colored lightbulbs for an even spookier look.

HALLOWEEN JAR LAMP

Recycled items: a thick plastic foam packing mold, large glass jar with lid (we used a 64-oz. pickle jar), five seedpods, white plastic bag, polyester fiberfill, twigs, and a paper or plastic lampshade

You will also need craft knife; craft glue; Spanish moss; sheet moss; paintbrushes; orange, green, yellow, and brown acrylic paint; black permanent fine-point marker; five floral pins; wire cutters; pinking shears; clear nylon thread; hammer and awl; screwdriver; lamp kit for bottle base; black spray primer; kraft paper; removable tape; transfer paper; stylus; spray adhesive; glue stick (optional); and an upholstery needle.

Use craft glue for all gluing unless otherwise indicated. Allow craft glue, primer, and paint to dry after each application unless otherwise indicated.

1. Cut a circle from foam slightly smaller than diameter of mouth of jar. Apply craft glue to one side of foam circle. Glue circle to inside bottom of jar. Glue Spanish moss and sheet moss in bottom of jar, covering foam circle.

2. For pumpkins, paint seedpods orange and stems of seedpods green. Use marker to draw faces on pumpkins. Insert one pin in bottom of each pumpkin. Use wire cutters to cut head from each pin. Inserting pins into foam and gluing to secure, arrange pumpkins in bottom of jar.

3. For ghost, use pinking shears to cut a 6" dia. circle from bag. For head, place a small amount of fiberfill at center of circle. Leaving a tail for hanging, use thread to gather circle around fiberfill. Use marker to draw eyes.

4. For trees, cut twigs to fit in jar. Tie ghost to one tree; stretch a small amount of fiberfill in tree to make a spider web. Inserting bottoms of twigs into foam and gluing to secure, arrange trees in bottom of jar.

5. Use hammer and awl to punch a small hole at center of jar lid. Use screwdriver to enlarge hole to accommodate lamp kit. Apply primer to lid. Follow manufacturer's instructions to assemble lamp.

6. For lampshade cover, find seamline of shade. If shade does not have a seamline, draw a vertical line from top edge to bottom edge of shade.

7. Centering one edge of kraft paper on shade seamline, tape in place. Wrap paper around shade, extending 1" past seamline; tape to secure (Fig. 1).

Fig. 1

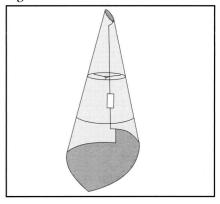

8. Using a pencil, lightly draw along top and bottom edges of shade. Draw a vertical line from top edge to bottom edge of shade 1/2" past seamline. Remove paper; use pinking shears to cut 1" outside drawn lines.

9. Enlarge moon, stars, and fence patterns, page 144, 133%; cut out. Use transfer paper and stylus to transfer patterns to cover, repeating patterns as desired. Paint moon and stars yellow and fence brown. Use black marker to outline designs; randomly mark dots for smaller stars on cover, then draw lines for starbursts emanating from each dot.

10. Matching straight edge of cover to seamline, use spray adhesive to adhere cover to shade. Make clips in top and bottom edges of cover to within 1/8" from shade edges; glue edges of cover to inside of shade.

11. Cutting through cover and shade and leaving shapes intact, use craft knife to cut around desired areas of moon and points of stars. Use upholstery needle to punch holes in centers of stars and through shade on dots.

"SPOOK-TACULAR" SPIDER

*G*ive *Halloween visitors a fright with this "spook-tacular" spider. It's easy! Just stuff his trash bag body full of assorted plastic bags, leaves, or crumpled paper. With spindly foam legs, this giant creepy-crawler is an impressive addition to your indoor or outdoor décor.*

PLASTIC SPIDER

Recycled items: four foam noodles with a solid center (swimming pool flotation toys; ours measure 2³/₄" in diameter), two rubber bands, assorted plastic bags (we used grocery and dry cleaning bags) or foam peanuts, four wire hangers, and two large black buttons

You will also need serrated knife, four 30-gal. black plastic trash bags, wire cutters, black electrical tape, low-temperature hot glue gun, and heavy-duty fishing line.

1. For each eye, use knife to cut a ¹/₂"-thick slice from one noodle; set aside.

2. Open one trash bag; gather bottom of bag, then wrap rubber band around gathers. Turn bag inside out; fill half way with plastic bags or foam peanuts.

3. Refer to Fig. 1 to cut and straighten hangers. Cut hook from three hangers; bend remaining hook to form a hanging loop. Referring to Assembly Diagram to arrange hangers, place hangers, one at a time, into bag, poking ends through opposite sides of bag; arrange hangers at center of bag and tape together to secure.

4. Cut each noodle in half to make eight legs. To make bends in each leg, mark halfway point on leg. Without cutting all the way through, use knife to cut away a wedge (about the size of an orange segment) at mark. Bend leg and secure with tape.

Fig. 1

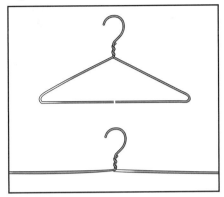

5. Cut three trash bags into 4"w strips. To cover each leg, start by covering one end, then wrap strips up around leg, securing with tape as needed.

6. Cut an opening in bag around each wire end sticking out from bag at each puncture point just large enough for end of each leg to slide through. Insert wire ends into legs; use tape to secure legs to body and to reinforce cuts in bag.

7. For each eye, glue a button on top of one foam slice, then glue eye to body.

8. To hang, knot a length of fishing line through hanging loop. Leaving about 5" at top, finish filling body with plastic bags or foam peanuts. Gather top of bag around hanging loop; wrap remaining rubber band around gathers. Cut bag above rubber band into strips for fringe.

ASSEMBLY DIAGRAM
TOP VIEW

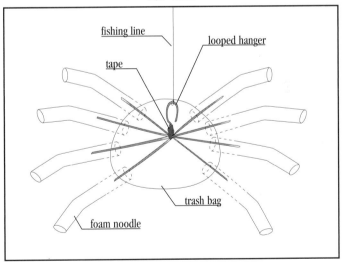

*L*et your little darling spread her wings this Halloween with a brilliant butterfly costume. A plastic-bag ruffle trims the colorful vinyl-tablecloth wings, and a bug-eyed hat with curly antennae caps off this winged wonder. Up, up, and away!

TABLECLOTH BUTTERFLY COSTUME

Recycled items: a 60" round vinyl tablecloth, felt scrap, plastic bags (we used yellow newspaper delivery bags), two 3-liter bottle caps, plastic foam bowl, and two twisted paper gift bag handles with wire centers

You will also need black permanent fine-point marker; transparent tape; thick craft glue; paintbrushes; black, ivory, and yellow acrylic paint; craft knife; hot glue gun; and 1 yd of 1³/₄"w ribbon.

Allow craft glue and paint to dry after each application.

1. For wings, fold vinyl tablecloth in half twice. Referring to Fig. 1, use marker to draw cutting lines for wings and neck opening. Cut through all layers along drawn lines.

Fig. 1

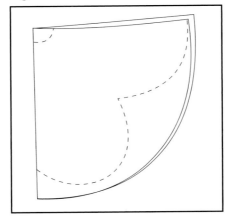

2. For body, enlarge pattern, page 145, 118%; make two photocopies, then cut out. Tape pieces together along blue line to make whole pattern. Using pattern, cut body from felt. Glue body to center front of wings.

3. Cut 1¹/₂"w strips from bags for ruffles. Gathering strips as you go, sew strips along edges of wings. Sew front and back of wings together under each arm.

4. For eyes, paint bottle caps black, then add ivory highlights. Press caps against outside of bowl to make indentions for placement of eyes. Using craft knife, cut out holes; insert eyes and hot glue to secure.

5. For antennae, curl ends of paper bag handles around pencil; paint yellow. Use pencil to punch two holes in bowl. Push ends of antennae through holes and bend to inside; hot glue to secure.

6. Use craft knife to cut two narrow 1³/₄"-long slits ¹/₈" apart on each side of hat. Beginning at inside and leaving long streamers, thread ribbon through slits on one side, then through opposite side; hot glue center of ribbon inside as necessary to secure.

STYLISH GIFT DRESSINGS

*C*lassy marbleized gift dressings give any present a polished look. Graceful wrap is crafted from brown paper bags and spray paint, while matching tags are made from manila folders and cereal box liners. You'll love this elegant, yet economical, gift wrap.

MARBLEIZED PAPER FOR GIFT WRAP AND TAGS

Recycled items: a large brown paper bag, large container (we used a long plastic planter and plugged the holes), manila folder, and a waxed-paper cereal box liner

You will also need desired colors of spray paint, clear acrylic spray sealer, decorative-edged craft scissors, fine-point permanent marker, craft glue, and a hole punch.

Note: Wearing rubber gloves is recommended when pulling paper from water to protect hands from paint.

1. For gift wrap, cut paper bag along seam and remove bottom.

2. Fill container with water. Rolling bag as necessary, immerse paper in water. Hold paper to one side of container, and spray a light layer of desired paints onto surface of water. Slowly unroll and pull paper from water, allowing paint to cling to paper; continue process until paper is coated. Hang to dry. Spray painted surface of paper with sealer and allow to dry.

3. For gift tags, cut manila folder in half along fold. Using painting technique in Step 2, paint folder pieces.

4. From painted folder, cut a 3" x 4¼" piece to make card, or a 4" square to make window tag.

5. For card, fold card piece in half, trim front edge with craft scissors, then write message on card.

6. For window tag, fold square piece in half; trim one end to a point. Cut an opening in one side of tag. Glue a piece of cereal box liner over opening on inside of tag, then glue edges of tag together. Punch hole in tag and write message.

PLACE CARD PARTY FAVORS

*L*ooking for a clever idea for your next dinner party? These delightful boxes do double-duty as place card holders and party favors. Just cover small containers with pretty wrapping paper scraps and tuck tiny treats inside. With personalized tags, these favors are terrific for making guests feel special!

PAPER-COVERED BOXES

Recycled items: small cardboard boxes with lids (we used a jewelry gift box and a face powder box) and wrapping paper scraps

You will also need spray adhesive, craft glue stick, card stock, 1/4" dia. hole punch, self-adhesive hole reinforcements, black permanent fine-point marker, favors to place in boxes, and jute twine or ribbon.

1. Using spray adhesive and glue stick as necessary, cover each box and lid with wrapping paper.

2. Cut tag shape from card stock. Punch hole in tag and add hole reinforcement. Use marker to write name on tag. Cut motif from wrapping paper and glue to tag.

3. Place favor in box. Tie a length of jute or ribbon around box. Thread tag onto one streamer, then tie streamers into a bow.

ITTY-BITTY GIFT BOXES

*E*ven the tiniest gift seems extraordinary when you present it in a charming little box, custom made from items you already have at home. Create the itty-bitty boxes from old greeting cards, then embellish with ribbon. Lots of other pretty paper products can be used, too, such as card stock, heavy weight stationery, or wrapping paper.

RECYCLED CARDS GIFT BOXES

Recycled items: greeting cards

You will also need a hot glue gun, gifts to place in boxes, ribbon, hole punch, and grommets and a setter.

1. Enlarge desired box pattern, page 146 – 147, to fit on card; cut out. Draw around pattern on back of card. Referring to lines on pattern, cut sections on solid lines and use a ruler to fold card along dashed lines. Fold card into a box and glue sides, as necessary.

2. For square box, place gift in box, then tie a length of ribbon into a bow around box.

3. For rectangular box, use hole punch and follow manufacturer's instructions to attach grommets where indicated on pattern. Place gift in box, then thread a length of ribbon through grommets to close; tie ribbon into a bow.

CREATIVE GIFT TOTE

*A*ny gift is twice as nice when it comes in this pretty present holder. Cut a lightweight cardboard box to resemble a tote bag with handles, then paint and embellish with coordinating greeting card cut-outs. Top with a colorful bow for a smart and speedy gift box that's guaranteed to please.

CUT-OUT GIFT BOX

Recycled items: a cardboard box (we used a 10" x 5" x 2½" box) and two coordinating greeting cards of different sizes (we layered a card with an illustration over a card with a floral border)

You will also need tracing paper, craft knife and cutting mat, white spray primer, paintbrushes, assorted colors of acrylic paint to coordinate with cards, spray adhesive, decorative-edge craft scissors, hot glue gun, and ribbon.

Allow primer and paint to dry after each application.

1. Adjusting width and length as necessary to fit box, trace handle pattern, page 148, onto tracing paper; cut out. Determine finished height of gift box, then draw around pattern on box front and back.

2. Mark straight across sides of box at base of handle. Cutting around handles, cut top and sides from box. Cut out center of handles.

3. Apply primer to inside and outside of box. Paint box desired color.

4. Use spray adhesive to adhere front card to center of background card. Trim edge of background card with craft scissors. Hot glue cards to front of box.

5. Paint designs on box to coordinate with cards.

6. Tie ribbon into a bow; hot glue bow to handle.

ROYAL FORTRESS

Transform an ordinary party into a magical world of wizards, knights, and princes with this stately centerpiece. Constructed from assorted boxes and containers, our remarkable castle will captivate a roomful of imaginative youngsters. Complete the magical aura by personalizing your fortress with the birthday boy's age and first initial.

CARDBOARD CASTLE CENTERPIECE

Recycled items: two metal bottle caps, cardboard box for castle (we used a $4^{1}/_{4}$" x $8^{3}/_{4}$" x $12^{1}/_{4}$" shoebox with a side-hinged lid and glued the lid closed), two round cardboard snack containers for towers (ours measure $5^{1}/_{8}$" dia. x $9^{1}/_{2}$"h), lightweight cardboard, scraps of gold trim, gold chain necklace or bracelets, two party hats, and an acrylic jewel

You will also need a hammer; white spray primer; grey spray paint; tracing paper; red, blue, and light blue felt; craft knife and cutting mat; paintbrush; black acrylic paint; gold paint pen; craft glue; awl; wire cutters; brass paper fasteners; and two metallic party sprays.

Allow primer, paint, and craft glue to dry after each application.

1. Use hammer to flatten bottle caps. Apply primer to castle, towers, and caps. Paint towers and castle grey, allowing some of the primer to show through.

2. Draw a $4^{1}/_{4}$" x $5^{1}/_{4}$" door on castle.

3. Trace window and banner patterns, page 148, onto tracing paper; cut out. Draw around window pattern on each side of door and on each tower (bottom of container is top of tower). Using banner pattern, cut two banners from red felt. Cut child's initial from red felt and numbers for child's age from blue felt.

4. For drawbridge, cut a $4^{1}/_{4}$" x $6^{1}/_{4}$" piece from cardboard. Score a line across cardboard piece 1" from one short edge, then fold along scored line.

5. Paint windows, door, and both sides of drawbridge black. Use paint pen to outline windows, door, and bottle caps.

6. Glue trim along front and side edges of drawbridge. Aligning fold of bridge with bottom edge of door, glue flap of bridge to bottom of castle. To attach chain, use awl to make holes through castle at sides of door and through bridge. Cut two lengths of chain; use paper fasteners to attach chain pieces to castle and drawbridge.

7. Use awl to make a hole in center of each cap and in center front of each party hat. Use paper fasteners to attach bottle caps to hats. Glue hats to tops of towers.

8. Glue initial above castle door; glue jewel to initial. Glue felt numbers to banners and banners to towers.

9. Cut a 1"w strip of blue felt long enough to fit around top of castle and one for each tower. Cut $^{1}/_{2}$" squares, $^{1}/_{2}$" apart from each felt strip to make "teeth." Glue strips around castle and towers. Insert one party spray into top of each hat; glue to secure.

10. Glue trim along top edges of banners, bottom edges of felt strips on each tower, and around top of each hat.

11. For moat, cut a large piece from light blue felt; place castle and towers at center of moat.

PARTY DOLL

*C*ap off a sleepover or birthday *party with a sweet country doll for each little girl. Cleverly made from small potato chip containers, each one houses a secret hiding place for treats and trinkets. Paint the flexible bottle-cap arms and legs to match a color theme, or alternate bottle caps with large, colorful buttons.*

BOTTLE CAP DOLL

Recycled items: round cardboard can with lid (ours measures $3^{1}/_{2}$"h x 3" dia.), fabric scraps, 42 metal bottle caps, assorted shank and flat buttons, child-size white sock, and a cardboard tag with hanger

You will also need spray adhesive, hammer and nail, desired color of spray paint (optional), wire cutters, 24-gauge red craft wire, hot glue gun, 2" dia. plastic foam ball, black and red permanent fine-point markers, pink colored pencil, and a 1" length of tan brush fringe.

1. Remove lid from can; set aside. For doll body, measure height of can between rims; add 1". Measure around can; add $^{1}/_{2}$". Cut a piece of fabric the determined measurements. Overlapping ends at back and folding excess fabric to inside of can, use spray adhesive to adhere fabric to body.

2. Use hammer and nail to punch a hole in center of can lid and each bottle cap, then punch holes in body for arms and legs.

3. Paint bottle caps, if desired, and allow to dry.

4. Cut five 8" lengths of wire. For each limb, thread one length of wire through desired shank button, then thread both ends of wire length through ten bottle caps. Thread wire ends through hole in body; twist ends and flatten inside can to secure. Cover ends with hot glue.

5. For head, place foam ball in toe of sock. Leaving a 4" tail, use remaining wire length to tightly gather sock around ball; twist ends to secure. Cut sock away below wire. Use black marker to draw eyes and mouth and colored pencil to blush cheeks. Glue fringe to head for hair. Cut a $7^{1}/_{2}$" triangle from fabric. Tie triangle around head for kerchief.

6. To attach head to "neck," thread tail of wire through remaining two bottle caps, then through hole in can lid, twisting wire and inside lid to secure. Cover wire ends with hot glue. Place head on body.

7. Use black and red markers to write on tag. Glue two buttons to front of body and one near neck. Hang tag from button at neck.

STARRY TOPIARY

*O*ur fanciful topiary gives a lonely nook a stellar new look! It's easy to create this miniature tree from common household discards. Sand or gravel anchors your topiary in a dressed-up tissue box, while recycled potpourri pieces, like pinecones or dried orange slices, are lovely embellishments. Muted colors make this a cozy complement for any décor.

NATURAL TOPIARY TREE

Recycled items: a boutique-style tissue box, twigs, rubber bands, plastic grocery bag, sand or gravel, twist tie, cardboard, and bubble wrap with small bubbles, dried orange slices, and miniature pinecones

You will also need spray primer, paintbrushes, dark red and dark brown acrylic paints, plastic wrap, utility scissors, hot glue gun, spray adhesive, sheet moss, raffia, Spanish moss, and 1¹/₂"w ribbon.

Allow primer and paint to dry after each application unless otherwise indicated.

1. Prime, then paint box red. Mix two parts brown paint to one part water. Working on one side at a time, brush mixture over box; while wet, pounce with crunched plastic wrap.

2. For stem, cut twigs into 21" lengths; secure together at top and bottom with rubber bands.

3. Place plastic bag in box and drape over the sides. Fill box one-third full with sand. Insert stem into box, then fill in around stem with sand. Gather bag around stem and secure with twist tie; trim excess bag.

4. Enlarge star pattern, page 139, 125%; cut out. Use pattern to cut two stars from cardboard. Hot glue points of stars together. Insert stem between stars and glue to secure.

5. Cover star with a layer of bubble wrap; hot glue to secure. Use spray adhesive to adhere sheet moss to bubble wrap.

6. Wrap and tie raffia around star. Glue Spanish moss, an orange slice, and pinecones to center of each side.

7. Securing with hot glue, cover top of box with Spanish moss, then sheet moss. Tie ribbon into a bow around box; trim ends.

119

FROSTY FLEECE PALS

Bundled-up snowman buckets are wonderfully easy ways to greet winter. Just fill with peppermints and place on tables throughout the house for handy treats. Everyone will love these playful and practical fleece-covered containers!

FLEECE-COVERED CAN SNOWMEN

Recycled items: small and large cardboard cans, pink powder blush, and assorted fabric scraps

You will also need orange polymer clay, 20-gauge craft wire, wire cutters, clear acrylic spray sealer, hot glue gun, poster board, white polyester fleece, pinking shears, assorted black pom-poms, black permanent fine-point marker, nail, polyester fiberfill, and chenille stems.

1. For each snowman, shape a nose from clay. Fold a 2" length of wire in half; push fold into base of nose, leaving $^1/_2$" of ends extending beyond nose. Follow clay manufacturer's instructions to bake nose; allow to cool, then apply sealer.

2. Glue a piece of poster board around can.

3. To cover can with fleece, measure around can and add $^1/_2$". Measure height of can; double measurement. Cut a piece of fleece the determined measurements. Overlapping ends at back, glue fleece around can.

4. Glue pom-poms to can for eyes and mouth. Apply powder blush for cheeks. Use marker to draw eyebrows.

5. To attach nose, use nail to punch a small hole through can at desired position. Apply a small amount of glue around edges of hole and insert wire ends at base of nose through hole. Spread wire ends on inside of can to secure nose; cover ends with glue. Fold excess fleece to inside of can. Glue in place.

6. For scarf, tear a $1^1/_2$"w strip of fabric long enough to tie around can; fray ends. Knot scarf around base of can.

7. For each earmuff, work *Running Stitches*, page 153, along edges of $4^1/_2$" dia. circle of fabric for small can or $5^1/_2$" dia. circle of fabric for large can. Place a small ball of fiberfill on wrong side of circle. Pull threads to gather edges of fabric over fiberfill; knot and trim ends.

8. For handle, glue ends of a chenille stem to sides of can; glue earmuffs over ends of handle.

SHIMMERING CD ORNAMENT

*T*urn a couple of junk mail CDs into a jolly memento! Start by gluing two discarded discs together. Then attach an image cut from a Christmas card to one side and a poetic greeting to the other. Iridescent glitter and glossy paint add sparkle to this whimsical wonder.

CD CHRISTMAS ORNAMENT

Recycled items: two compact discs and Christmas cards

You will also need clear nylon thread, wood glue, craft glue stick, paintbrushes, assorted colors of acrylic paints, card stock, decorative-edge craft scissors, and fine iridescent glitter (optional).

Use craft glue stick for all gluing unless otherwise indicated. Allow glue and paint to dry after each application.

1. For hanger, knot ends of a 10" length of clear thread together. Spread wood glue over printed sides of discs. Place knot of hanger between edges of discs and press discs firmly together.

2. Cut design from front of one Christmas card; glue design to ornament.

3. Paint details on ornament as desired.

4. Cut greeting from inside of card and glue to card stock; cut around greeting with craft scissors. Glue greeting to back of ornament.

Tip: *If you've cut off some of the design of your card, you can paint it on the ornament. Add some glitter to the details before they dry.*

ORNAMENTAL BLOCK

*G*olden angels adorn our ethereal ornament and keep watch over your Christmas tree. No one will ever guess that this elegant accent is really a milk carton embellished with old Christmas cards. Create a single theme with coordinating pictures like we did or mix and match various types of cards and photos for a more eclectic look.

MILK CARTON ORNAMENT

Recycled items: one-pint beverage carton, clear plastic take-out container, Christmas cards, and trims

You will also need craft glue.

Allow glue to dry after each application.

1. Open top of carton. Measure width of carton bottom. Draw a line around carton this distance from bottom edge. Cut down corners of carton to drawn line. Cutting away excess, fold side flaps inward along drawn lines and glue in place to form cube.

2. Cut a square $1/8$" smaller than width of carton bottom from take-out container. For image on each side of ornament, place square over card until desired area is centered within edges of square, then draw around square on card; cut out. Center and glue images to cube.

3. Making a loop past one corner of cube for hanger, glue trim along each section.

> *Tip:* To ensure card images on cube are facing the desired direction when ornament is hanging, use a straight pin to mark corner of cube for hanger placement before gluing images in place.

ANGELIC SNOWMAN TREE TOPPER

*O*ur simple snowman will look angelic atop your Yuletide tree. Create his body from cast-off lids of various sizes. Sheer wings are made from panty hose and a wire coat hanger, and a shimmering chenille stem halo crowns this friendly snow angel. Assorted buttons complete the sweet ensemble.

LID SNOWMAN TREE TOPPER

Recycled items: three can lids in graduated sizes (we used 3³/₄" dia., 4" dia., and 6¹/₈" dia. lids cut from can using a safety can opener), white wire clothes hanger, panty hose, and assorted orange and black buttons

You will also need sandpaper, tack cloth, white spray primer, white spray paint, household cement, wire cutters, pliers, craft glue, silver glitter, silver chenille stem, and a heart-shaped button.

Use household cement for all gluing unless otherwise indicated. Allow primer, paint, and household cement to dry after each application.

1. Lightly sand lids; wipe with tack cloth. Apply primer, then paint lids.

2. Overlapping lids, glue together to form snowman.

3. For wings, cut hanger at center bottom. Referring to Wings Diagram, use pliers to bend hanger into wings and arms. Trimming as necessary and knotting at center to secure, slide panty hose over wings.

4. Paint wings white. Outline wings with craft glue, then sprinkle with glitter; allow to dry, then shake off excess glitter. Glue wings to back of body.

5. Form one end of chenille stem into a halo. Glue stem of halo to back of head.

6. Glue graduated sizes of orange buttons together to form nose; glue in place. Glue black buttons to face for eyes and mouth; glue heart-shaped button and three black buttons to front of snowman.

WINGS DIAGRAM

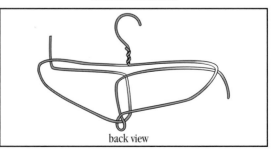

back view

JOLLY SNOWMAN CANDLEHOLDER

*A*dd a warm glow to a cold winter's eve with this clever candleholder! Simply paint a snowy scene on a glass jar and fit a tapered juice glass in the opening. Enhance with a cheerful bow, and you've got the perfect container for a fragrant candle.

DRINKING GLASS CANDLEHOLDER JAR

Recycled items: a canning jar (at least 7" tall), toothbrush, strip of fabric, and a small drinking glass that sits in opening of jar

You will also need paintbrushes; blue, white, red, black, orange, yellow, and green acrylic paint; small round spouncer; tracing paper; stylus; light colored transfer paper; black permanent fine-point marker; and a candle to fit in drinking glass.

Refer to Painting Techniques, page 151, before beginning project. Allow paint to dry after each application.

1. Apply two coats of blue paint to jar. Use spouncer to add a 1¹⁄₂" to 2"-high snowdrift along bottom of jar. *Spatter Paint* jar white.

2. Trace snowman pattern, page 150, onto tracing paper. Use stylus and transfer paper to transfer snowman to jar.

3. Paint snowman white, hat and scarf red, black *Dots* for eyes and buttons, and an orange nose. Paint yellow stars and add yellow stripes to scarf; paint green holly on hat.

4. Using marker, outline snowman. Use spouncer to lightly *Sponge Paint* white over outline to soften lines.

5. Tie strip of fabric into a bow around top of jar. Place glass in jar opening; place candle in glass.

125

Put the spotlight on creativity this Christmas season with lustrous glass trimmings. Just use paint markers and dots of dimensional paint to accent old lightbulbs. These original ornaments will give your Yuletide tree an artful touch. How enlightening!

LIGHTBULB ORNAMENTS

Recycled items: lightbulbs (we used standard bulbs, small appliance bulbs, and candelabra bulbs)

You will also need rubbing alcohol, painter's masking tape, paintbrushes, paint for basecoats (we used assorted colors of glass paint and stained glass spray finish), paint for decorative accents (we used assorted dimensional paints, assorted opaque paint and pigment pens), 24-gauge gold craft wire, wire cutters, clear satin acrylic spray sealer or glitter spray finish, sponges, glazing medium, and wax paper.

Refer to Painting Techniques, page 151, before beginning projects. Allow paint and sealer to dry after each application. Clean all bulbs with alcohol before painting.

DOTTED ORNAMENTS

1. Mask metal base of bulb above glass.

2. Paint bulbs desired basecoat color. Use dimensional paint to cover bulbs with dots. Remove tape, then use paint pen to paint base; apply sealer.

3. For hanger, wrap one end of wire around base of bulb; create a handle, wrap opposite end around base, then twist around itself to secure.

DOTTED RING ORNAMENT

1. Use dimensional paint to make lines around bulb. When dry, paint dots along lines.

2. Use glitter spray finish to paint base; apply sealer.

3. For hanger, wrap one end of wire around base of bulb; create a handle, wrap opposite end around base, then twist around itself to secure.

SWIRL ORNAMENTS

1. Mask metal base of bulb above glass and if desired, bottom section of bulb.

2. Apply basecoat to bulbs as desired; use paint pens to make swirls on bulbs. If desired, add dimensional paint dots around swirls.

3. Remove tape, then use paint pen to paint base; apply sealer.

4. For hanger, wrap one end of wire around base of bulb; create a handle, wrap opposite end around base, then twist around itself to secure.

DOTTED DESIGN ORNAMENTS

1. Mask metal base of bulb above glass.

2. *Sponge Paint* bulb desired basecoat color. Use dimensional paint and paint pens to embellish. Remove tape, then use paint pen to paint base; apply sealer.

3. For hanger, wrap one end of wire around base of bulb; create a handle, wrap opposite end around base, then twist around itself to secure.

TEXTURED ORNAMENT

1. Mask metal base of bulb above glass.

2. *Sponge Paint* bulb desired basecoat color. Using mixture of one part gold paint and one part glazing medium, paint bulb. While wet, dab with crumpled wax paper, until desired texture is achieved.

3. Remove tape, then use paint pen to paint base; apply sealer.

4. For hanger, wrap one end of wire around base of bulb; create a handle, wrap opposite end around base, then twist around itself to secure.

PATRIOTIC
PAPER
COLLAGE
(page 9)

A picture is worth a thousand words.

top

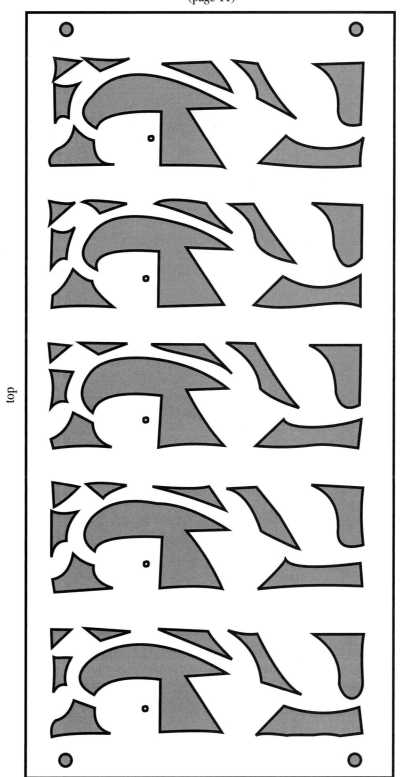

PATTERNS (continued)

SODA-CAN PALM TREE AND
PENCIL HUT

(page 13)

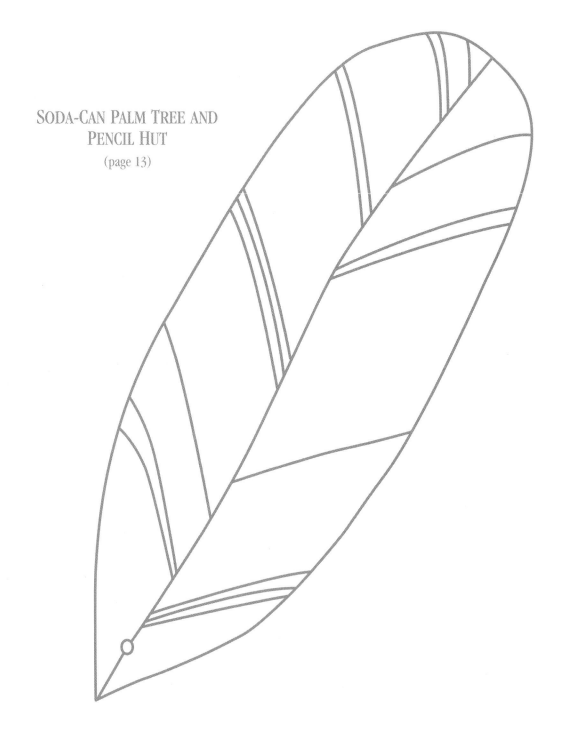

DENIM-COVERED WALL LETTERS
(page 18)

WRISTWATCH WALL CLOCK
(page 21)

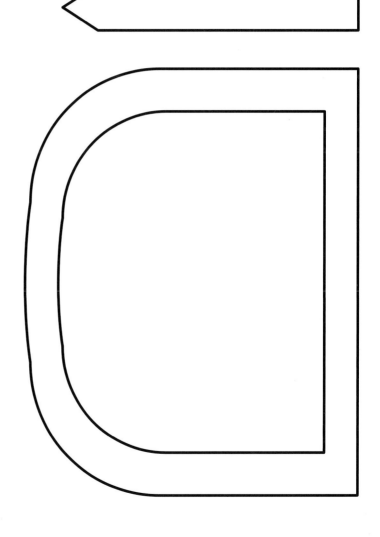

STAMPED FLORALS
(page 23)

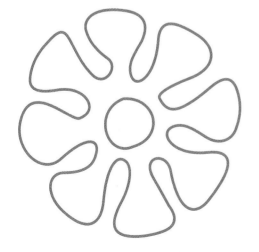

PATTERNS (continued)

BROWN PAPER FRAME

(page 28)

Having a great time...

Wish I were here

COFFEE CAN TABLE AND SODA-CAN VINE

(page 27)

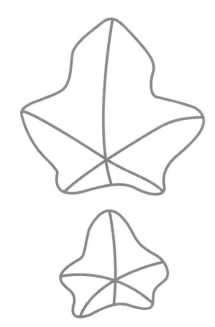

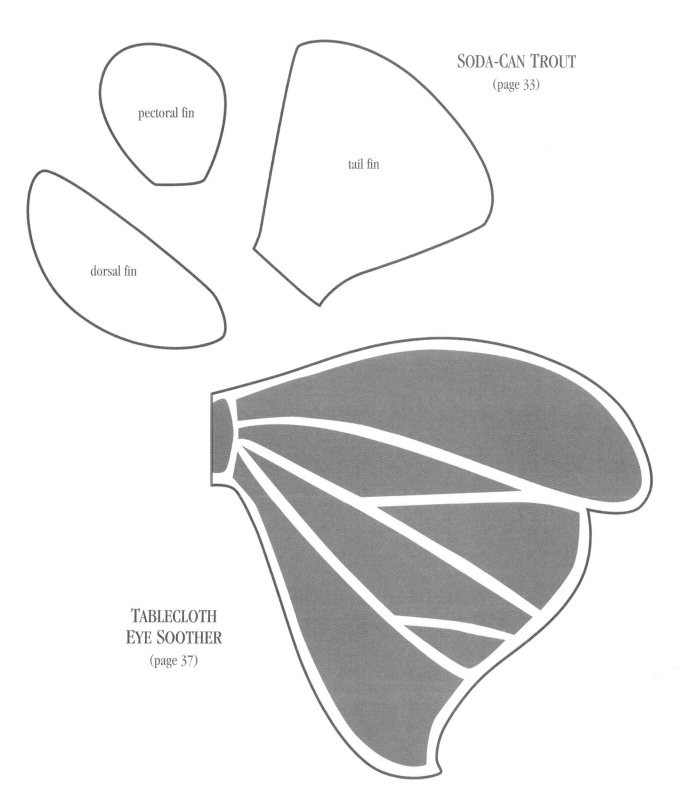

pectoral fin

tail fin

SODA-CAN TROUT
(page 33)

dorsal fin

**TABLECLOTH
EYE SOOTHER**
(page 37)

CHENILLE AND SOCK SCRAPS LAMB

(page 39)

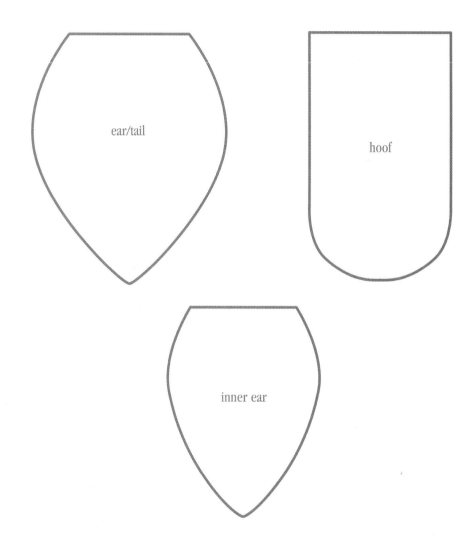

ear/tail

hoof

inner ear

ALUMINUM CAN FLOWER PLANT POKES
(page 55)

rose   red weed   daisy   blue weed   pansy

PATTERNS (continued)

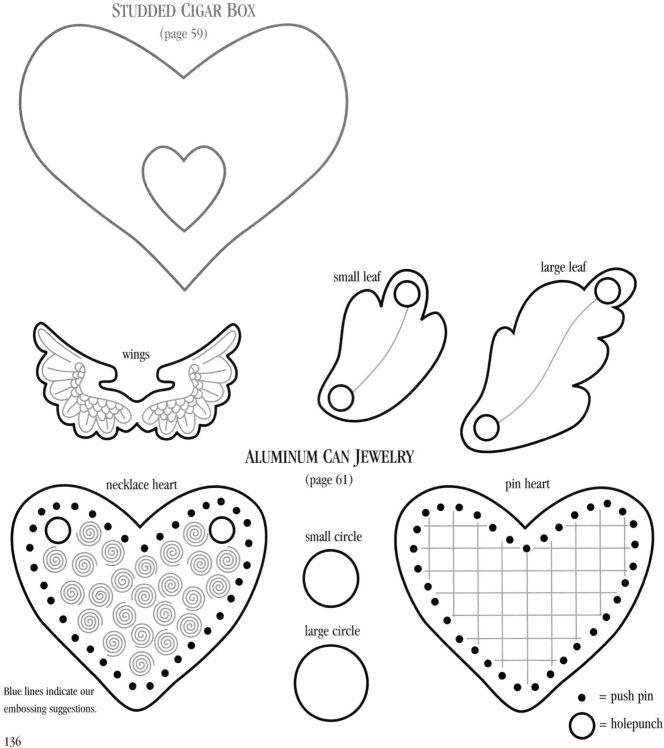

STUDDED CIGAR BOX
(page 59)

small leaf

large leaf

wings

ALUMINUM CAN JEWELRY
(page 61)

necklace heart

small circle

large circle

pin heart

Blue lines indicate our embossing suggestions.

• = push pin

◯ = holepunch

SHREDDED PAPER VASE
(page 67)

BOOK COVER FRAME
(page 68)

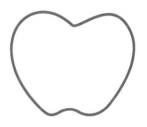

MATCHBOX PENDANT
(page 62)

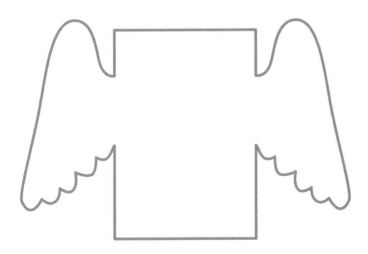

PATTERNS (continued)

COFFEE CAN LUMINARY
(page 75)

PLASTIC BOTTLE BIRDHOUSES
(page 73)

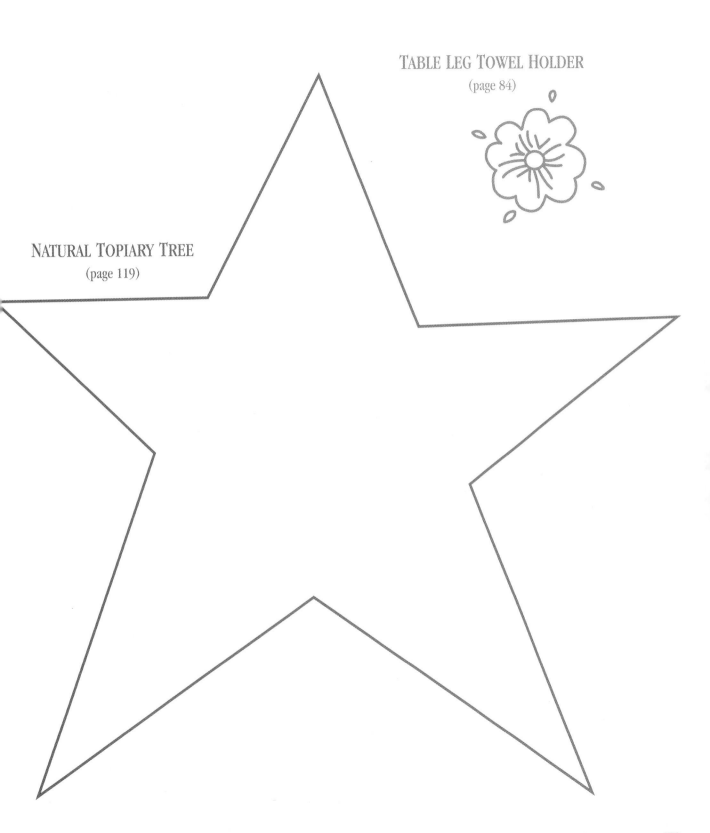

TABLE LEG TOWEL HOLDER
(page 84)

NATURAL TOPIARY TREE
(page 119)

139

PATTERNS (continued)

CAN EMBELLISHED FRAMES
(page 89)

CAP-STUDDED SERVING CRATE
(page 88)

PAINTED STOOL
(page 85)

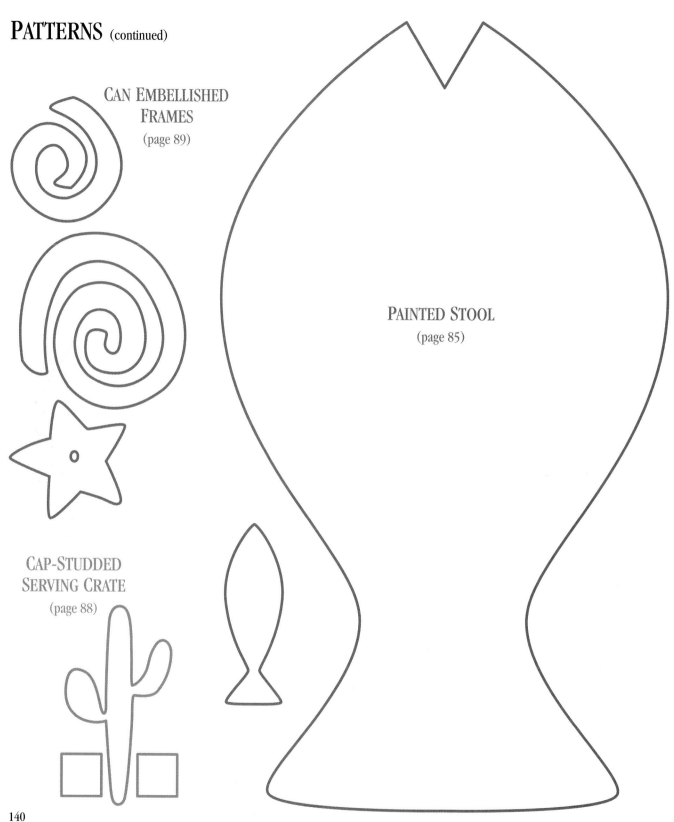

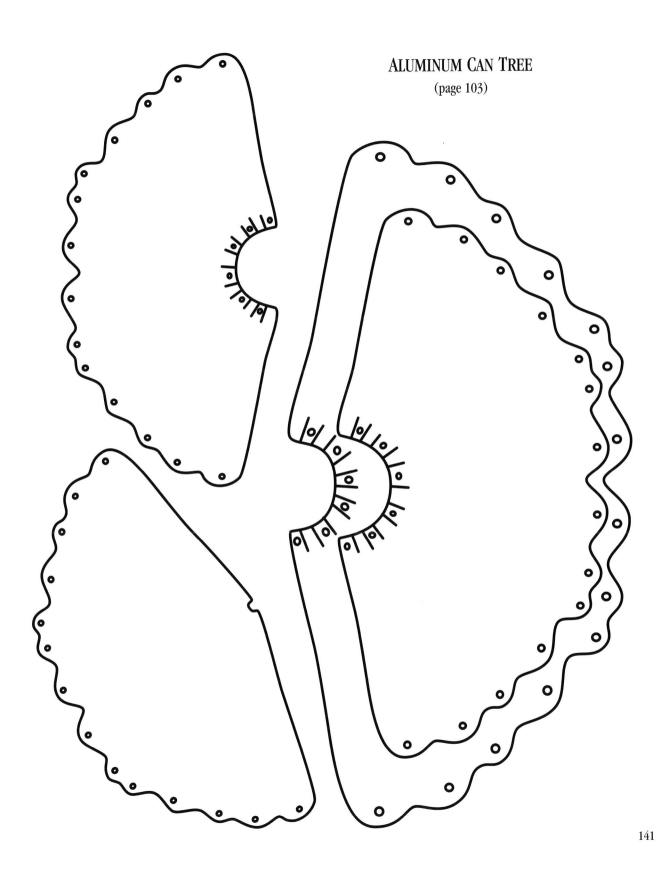

PATTERNS (continued)

PAINTED VINYL WALL HANGING
(page 104)

PLASTIC FOAM WREATH
(page 105)

PATTERNS (continued)

HALLOWEEN JAR LAMP
(page 107)

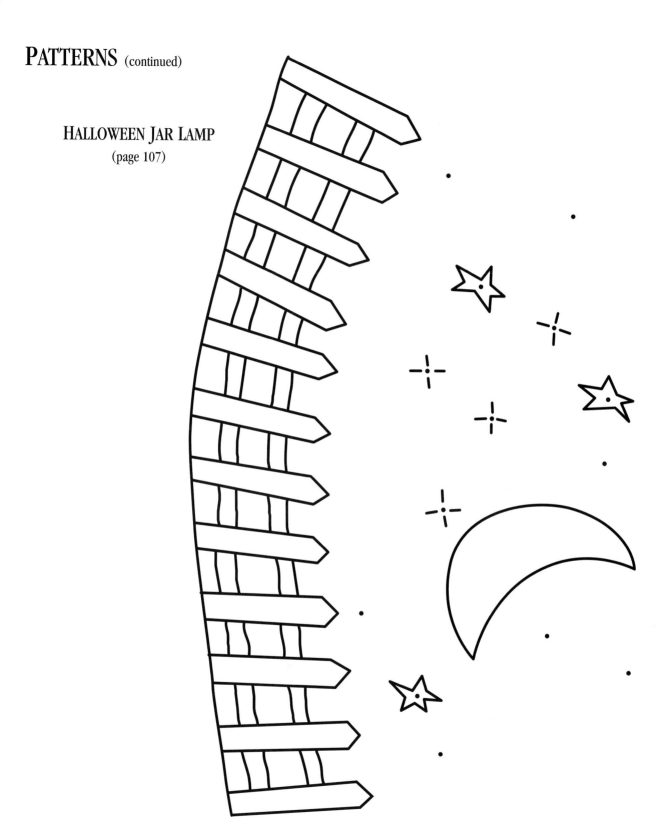

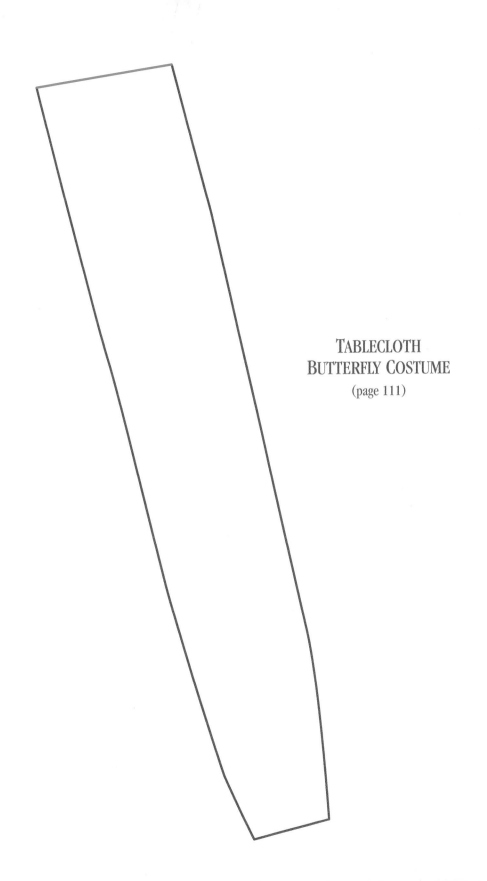

TABLECLOTH
BUTTERFLY COSTUME
(page 111)

PATTERNS (continued)

RECYCLED CARDS
GIFT BOXES
(page 114)

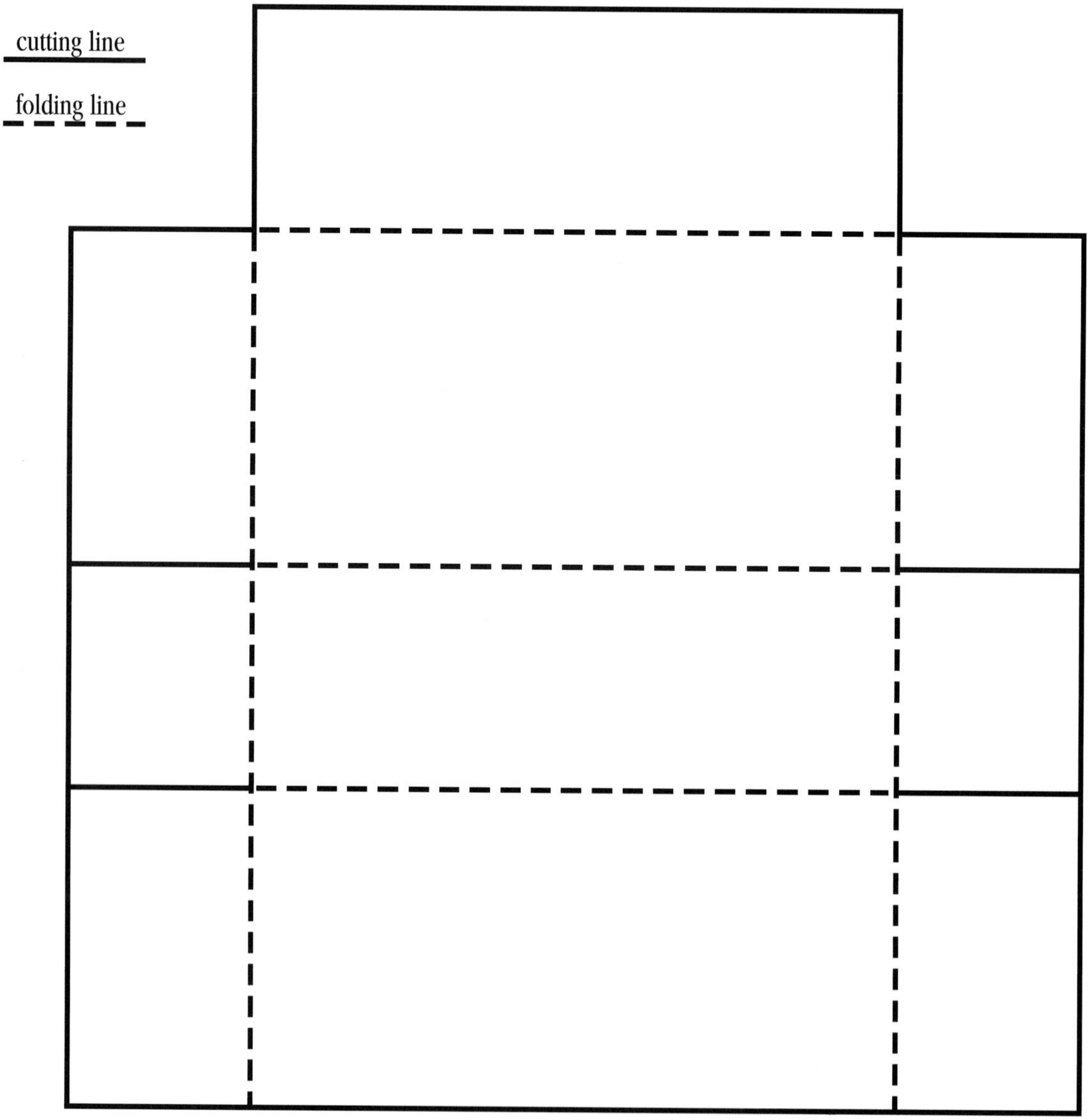

cutting line

folding line

cutting line

folding line

RECYCLED CARDS
GIFT BOXES
(page 114)

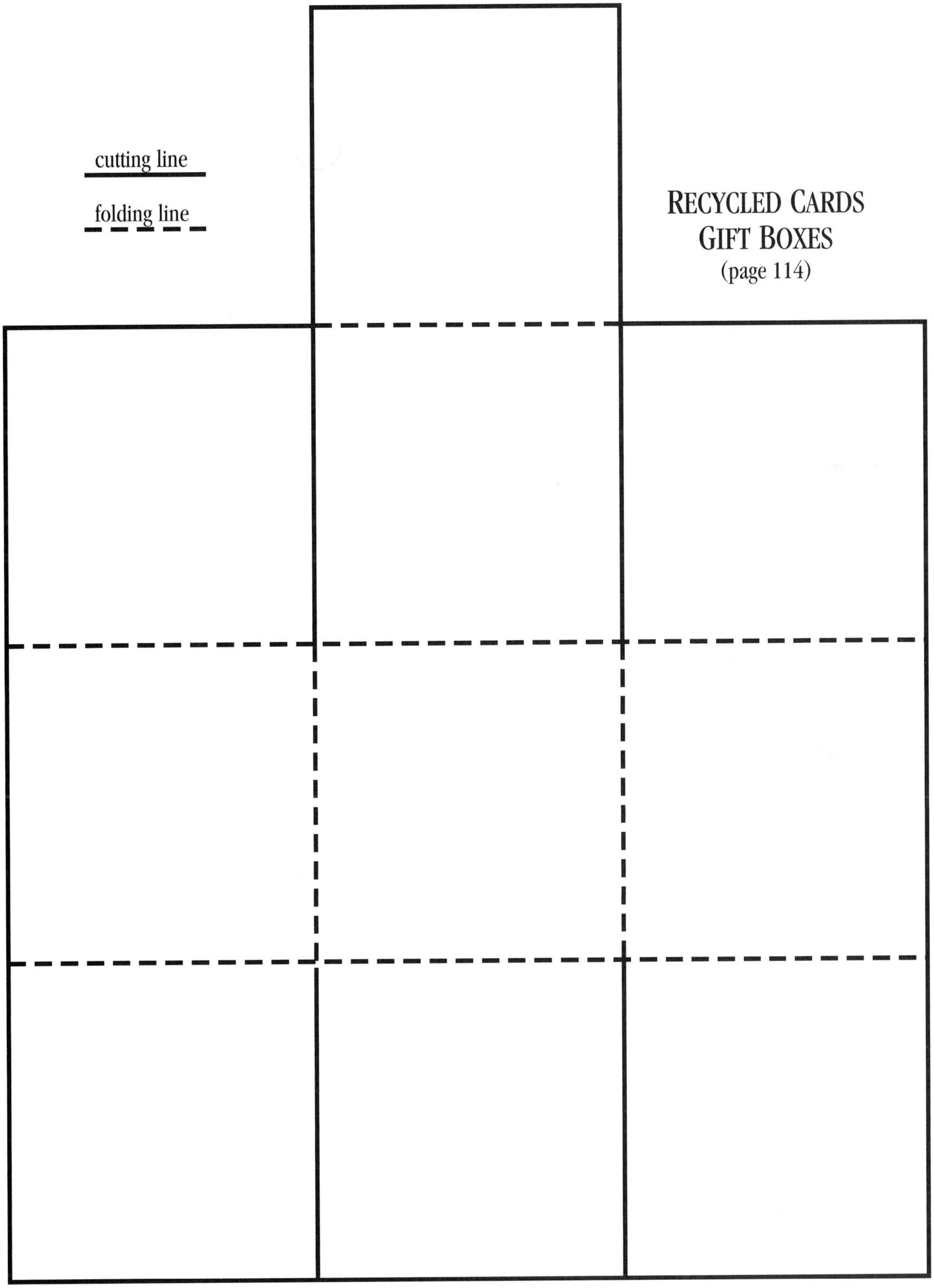

PATTERNS (continued)

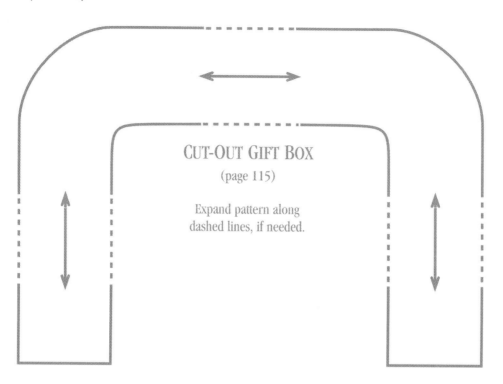

CUT-OUT GIFT BOX

(page 115)

Expand pattern along
dashed lines, if needed.

CARDBOARD CASTLE
CENTERPIECE

(page 117)

window

banner

B

A

PATTERNS (continued)

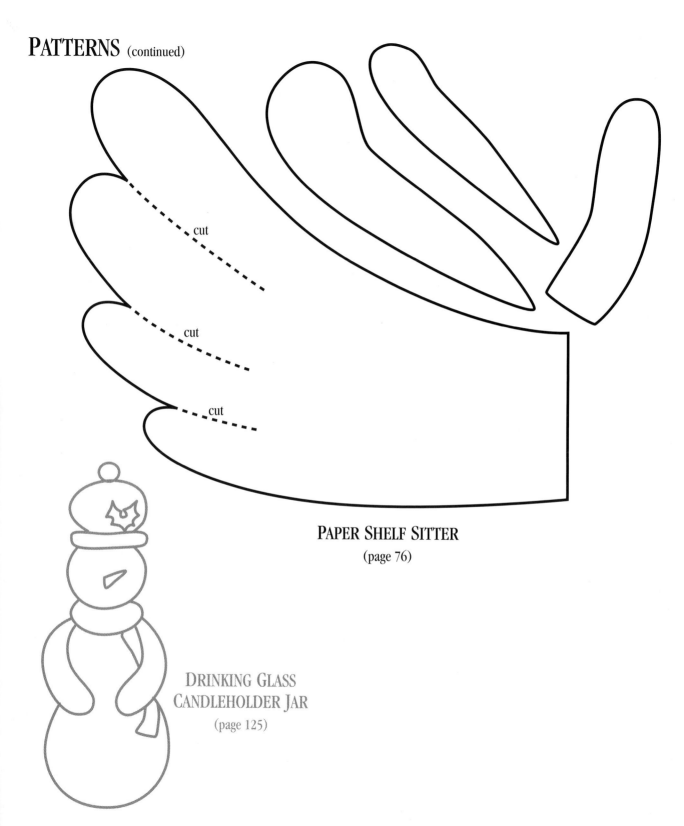

cut

cut

cut

PAPER SHELF SITTER

(page 76)

**DRINKING GLASS
CANDLEHOLDER JAR**

(page 125)

GENERAL INSTRUCTIONS

ADHESIVES

When using any adhesive, carefully follow the manufacturer's instructions.

White craft glue: Recommended for paper. Dry flat.

Tacky craft glue: Recommended for paper, fabric, florals, or wood. Dry flat or secure items with clothespins or straight pins until glue is dry.

Craft glue stick: Recommended for paper or for gluing small, lightweight items to paper or other surfaces. Dry flat.

Fabric glue: Recommended for fabric or paper. Dry flat or secure items with clothespins or straight pins until glue is dry.

Découpage glue: Recommended for découpaging fabric or paper to a surface such as wood or glass. Use purchased découpage glue or mix one part craft glue with one part water.

Hot or low-temperature glue gun: Recommended for paper, fabric, florals, or wood. Hold in place until set.

Rubber cement: Recommended for paper and cardboard. May discolor photos; may discolor paper with age. Dry flat (dries very quickly).

Spray adhesive: Recommended for paper or fabric. Can be repositioned or permanent. Dry flat.

Household cement: Recommended for ceramic or metal. Secure items with clothespins until glue is dry.

Wood glue: Recommended for wood. Nail, screw, or clamp items together until glue is dry.

Silicone adhesive: Recommended for ceramic, glass, leather, rubber, wood, and plastics. Forms a flexible and waterproof bond.

PAINTING TECHNIQUES

A disposable foam plate makes a good palette for holding and mixing paint colors. It can easily be placed in a large resealable plastic bag to keep remaining paint wet while waiting for an area of applied paint to dry.

When waiting for large areas to dry, before applying a second coat, wrap your paintbrush in plastic wrap and place in the refrigerator to keep paint from drying on your brush. Always clean brushes thoroughly after use to keep them in good condition.

TRANSFERRING A PATTERN

Trace pattern onto tracing paper. Place transfer paper, coated side down, between project and traced pattern. Use removable tape to secure pattern to project. Use a pencil to transfer outlines of design to project (press lightly to avoid smudges and heavy lines that are difficult to cover). If necessary, use a soft eraser to remove any smudges.

TRANSFERRING DETAILS

To transfer detail lines to design, position pattern and transfer paper over painted basecoat and use a pencil to lightly transfer detail lines onto project.

ADDING DETAILS

Use a permanent marker or paint pen (usually with a fine-tip) to draw over transferred detail lines or to create freehand details on project.

PAINTING BASECOATS

A basecoat is a solid color of paint that covers the project's entire surface.

Use a medium round brush for large areas and a small round brush for small areas. Do not overload brush. Allowing to dry between coats, apply several thin coats of paint to project.

DOTS

Dip handle end of paintbrush for larger dots or the end of a toothpick for smaller dots, into paint; touch to painting surface and lift straight up. Dip tip into paint frequently to maintain uniform dots.

DRY BRUSH

This technique creates a random top coat coloration of a project surface. It is similar to a color wash, yet creates an aged look that sits on top of the project's surface.

Do not dip brush in water. Dip a stipple brush or old paintbrush in paint; wipe most of the paint off onto a dry paper towel. Lightly rub the brush across the area to receive color. Decrease pressure on the brush as you move outward. Repeat as needed to create the desired coverage of color.

RUSTING

This technique creates a faux-rusted finish on project's surface.

1. Spray surface of project with a rust-colored primer.

2. For paints, unevenly mix one part water to one part orange acrylic paint; unevenly mix one part water to one part dark orange acrylic paint.

3. (*Note*: To create a more natural rusted look, use a paper towel or a clean damp sponge piece to dab off paint in some areas after applying paint. Also, drip a few drops of water onto painted surface while paint is still wet, let water run, and then allow to dry.) Dip a dampened sponge into paint; blot on paper towel to remove excess paint. Allowing to dry after each coat, use a light stamping motion to paint project with orange, then dark orange

GENERAL INSTRUCTIONS (continued)

paint mixtures. Apply sealer to project and allow to dry.

SPATTER PAINTING

This technique creates a speckled look on project's surface.

Dip the bristle tips of a dry toothbrush into paint, blot on a paper towel to remove excess, then pull thumb across bristles to spatter paint on project.

SPONGE PAINTING

This technique creates a soft, mottled look on project's surface.

1. Dampen sponge with water.

2. Dip dampened sponge into paint; blot on paper towel to remove excess paint.

3. Use a light stamping motion to paint project. Allow to dry.

4. If using more than one color of paint, repeat Steps 1 – 3, using a fresh sponge piece for each color.

5. If desired, repeat technique using one color again over areas of other colors, to soften edges or to lighten up a heavy application of one color.

STENCILING

These instructions are written for multicolor stencils. For single-color stencils, make one stencil for the entire design.

1. For first stencil, cut a piece from stencil plastic 1" larger than entire pattern. Center plastic over pattern and use a permanent pen to trace outlines of all areas of first color in stencil cutting key. For placement guidelines, outline remaining colored area using dashed lines. Using a new piece of plastic for each additional color in stencil cutting key, repeat for remaining stencils.

2. Place each plastic piece on cutting mat and use a craft knife to cut out stencil along solid lines, making sure edges are smooth.

3. Hold or tape stencil in place. Using a clean, dry stencil brush or sponge piece, dip brush or sponge in paint. Remove excess paint on a paper towel. Brush or sponge should be almost dry to produce best results. Beginning at edge of cutout area, apply paint in a stamping motion over stencil. If desired, highlight or shade design by stamping a lighter or darker shade of paint in cutout area. Repeat until all areas of first stencil have been painted. Carefully remove stencil and allow paint to dry.

4. Using stencils in order indicated in color key and matching guidelines on stencils to previously stenciled area, repeat Step 3 for remaining stencils.

MAKING PATTERNS

For a more durable pattern, use a permanent pen to trace pattern onto stencil plastic instead of tracing paper. Or cut out the tracing paper pattern, place it on cardboard, draw around it, and then cut out a cardboard pattern.

Place tracing paper over pattern and trace lines of pattern; cut out.

When only a half pattern is shown (indicated by a solid blue line on pattern), fold tracing paper in half. Place the fold along solid blue line and trace pattern half. Turn paper over and draw along pattern half. Open tracing paper and cut out whole pattern.

DÉCOUPAGE

1. Cut desired motifs from fabric or paper.

2. Apply découpage glue to wrong sides of motifs.

3. Arrange motifs on project as desired, overlapping as necessary. Smooth in place and allow to dry.

4. Allowing to dry after each application, apply two to three coats of sealer to project.

WORKING WITH WAX

MELTING WAX

Caution: Do not melt wax over an open flame or in a pan placed directly on burner.

1. Cover work area with newspaper.

2. Heat 1" of water in a saucepan to boiling. Add water as necessary.

3. Place wax in a large can. If pouring wax, pinch top rim of can to form a spout. If dipping candles, use a can 2" taller than height of candle to be dipped.

4. To melt wax, place can in boiling water and reduce heat to simmer. If color is desired, melt pieces of crayon or bits of wax color blocks in wax. Use a craft stick to stir, if necessary.

SETTING WICKS

1. Cut a length of wax-coated wick 1" longer than depth of candle container.

2. Using an oven mitt, carefully pour wax into container.

3. Allow wax to harden slightly and insert wick at center of candle. Allow wax to harden completely.

EMBROIDERY STITCHES

RUNNING STITCH
Make a series of straight stitches with stitch length equal to the space between stitches (Fig. 1).

Fig. 1

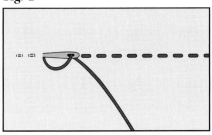

STRAIGHT STITCH
Bring needle up at 1 and go down at 2 (Fig. 2). Length of stitches may be varied as desired.

Fig. 2

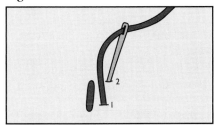

WHIPSTITCH
With right sides of folded fabric edges together, insert the needle through both folds, barely catching the edges. Following Fig. 3 take thread around folded edges of fabric and insert the needle close to the previous stitch through both folds; gently pull the thread to hold pieces together.

Fig. 3

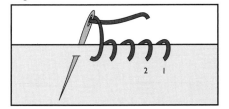

BLANKET STITCH
Bring needle up at 1; keeping thread below point of needle, go down at 2 and up at 3 (Fig. 4a). Continue working as shown in Fig. 4b.

Fig. 4a   **Fig. 4b**

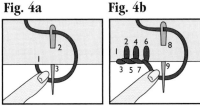

PAPER MAKING

1. Tear paper to be recycled into pieces about ¹/₂" square; place in bucket. Fill bucket with hot water and soak for at least one hour.

2. Wearing rubber gloves, squeeze excess water from a small handful of pre-soaked paper pieces and place in blender; cover with water until blender is half full. Blend at low speed for fifteen seconds, increasing speed to medium, then high, at fifteen second intervals; decrease speed in the same manner. When pulp is no longer lumpy, pour it into a second bucket.

3. With one handful of soaked paper pieces at a time, repeat the blending process until all pieces have been processed.

4. Lay a towel on a flat surface and cover with a piece of screen wire. Scoop pulp from bucket and press onto screen; place another piece of screen, then another towel on pulp and press to let towels absorb excess water. Use prepared pulp to complete project.

FUSIBLE APPLIQUÉS

To prevent darker fabrics from showing through, white or light-colored fabrics may need to be lined with fusible interfacing before applying paper-backed fusible web.

Follow all steps for each appliqué. When tracing patterns for more than one appliqué, leave at least 1" between shapes on web.

To make a reverse appliqué piece, trace pattern onto tracing paper; turn traced pattern over and continue to follow all steps using reversed pattern.

When an appliqué pattern contains shaded areas, trace along entire outer line for appliqué indicated in project instructions. Trace outer lines of shaded areas separately for additional appliqués indicated in project instructions.

Appliqués can be temporarily held in place by touching appliqués with tip of iron. If appliqués are not in desired position, lift and reposition.

1. Use a pencil to trace pattern onto paper side of web as many times as indicated in project instructions for a single fabric. Repeat for additional patterns and fabrics.

2. Follow manufacturer's instructions to fuse traced patterns to wrong side of fabrics. Do not remove paper backing.

3. Cut out appliqué pieces along traced lines. Remove paper backing.

4. Overlapping as necessary, arrange appliqués web side down on project.

5. Fuse appliqués in place.

CROCHET BASICS

ABBREVIATIONS

ch(s)   chain(s)

cm   centimeters

mm   millimeters

Rnd(s)   Round(s)

sc   single crochet(s)

st(s)   stitch(es)

( ) — work enclosed instructions **as many** times as specified by the number immediately following **or** contains explanatory remarks.

colon(:) — the number given after a colon at the end of a round denotes the number of stitches you should have on that round.

GAUGE

When crocheting with fabric strips, gauge isn't really important; your finished piece can be a little larger or smaller without changing the overall effect. However, your tension must be maintained throughout to keep piece laying flat.

FREE LOOPS OF A CHAIN

When instructed to work in free loops of a chain, work in loop indicated by arrow (Fig. 1).

Fig. 1

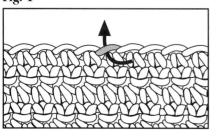

PREPARING FABRIC

Cut away all seams and hems. Remove stitching from any pockets and remove. Using scissors or a rotary cutter and mat, cut fabric into strips according to project instructions.

JOINING FABRIC STRIPS

The following is a technique for joining fabric strips without sewing strips together, and eliminates large knots or ends to weave in later.

1. To join a new strip of fabric to working strip, cut a 1" (2.5 cm) slit, about ¹/₂" (12 mm) from ends of both fabric strips (Fig. 2).

Fig. 2

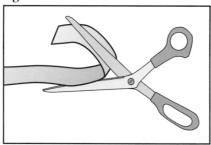

2. With **right** sides up, place end of new strip over end of working strip and match slits (Fig. 3).

Fig. 3

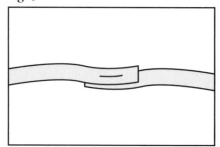

3. Pull free end of new strip through both slits from bottom to top (Fig. 4).

Fig. 4

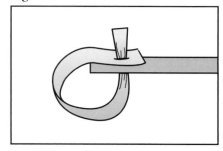

4. Pull new strip firmly to form a small knot (Fig. 5). Right sides of both strips should be facing up. Continue working with new strip.

Fig. 5

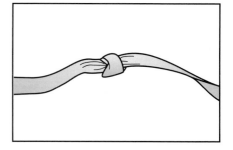

CHANGING COLORS

Instructions are written without color changes. To change colors, work the last stitch to last step (2 loops on hook); cut working strip to 1¹/₂" (4 cm), follow steps for Joining Fabric Strips to attach the new color strip, and complete the stitch with the new strip.

CROCHET RUG INSTRUCTIONS (continued from page 51)

Rnd 14: Ch 1, sc in same st and in next sc, 2 sc in next sc, sc in next 8 sc, 2 sc in next sc, sc in next 35 sc, 2 sc in next sc, (sc in next 8 sc, 2 sc in next sc) 3 times, sc in next 35 sc, 2 sc in next sc, sc in next 8 sc, 2 sc in next sc, sc in last 6 sc; join with slip st to first sc: 134 sc.

Rnd 15: Ch 1, sc in same st and in next 8 sc, 2 sc in next sc, sc in next 46 sc, 2 sc in next sc, (sc in next 9 sc, 2 sc in next sc) twice, sc in next 46 sc, 2 sc in next sc, sc in next 9 sc, 2 sc in last sc; join with slip st to first sc: 140 sc.

Rnd 16: Ch 1, sc in same st and in next 4 sc, 2 sc in next sc, sc in next 10 sc, 2 sc in next sc, sc in next 36 sc, 2 sc in next sc, (sc in next 10 sc, 2 sc in next sc) 3 times, sc in next 36 sc, 2 sc in next sc, sc in next 10 sc, 2 sc in next sc, sc in last 5 sc; join with slip st to first sc: 148 sc.

Rnd 17: Ch 1, sc in same st and in next 9 sc, 2 sc in next sc, sc in next 49 sc, 2 sc in next sc, (sc in next 11 sc, 2 sc in next sc) twice, sc in next 49 sc, 2 sc in next sc, sc in next 11 sc, 2 sc in next sc, sc in last sc; join with slip st to first sc: 154 sc.

Rnd 18: Ch 1, sc in same st and in next 4 sc, 2 sc in next sc, sc in next 12 sc, 2 sc in next sc, sc in next 37 sc, 2 sc in next sc, (sc in next 12 sc, 2 sc in next sc) 3 times, sc in next 37 sc, 2 sc in next sc, sc in next 12 sc, 2 sc in next sc, sc in last 7 sc; join with slip st to first sc: 162 sc.

Rnd 19: Ch 1, sc in same st and in next 11 sc, 2 sc in next sc, sc in next 52 sc, 2 sc in next sc, (sc in next 13 sc, 2 sc in next sc) twice, sc in next 52 sc, 2 sc in next sc, sc in next 13 sc, 2 sc in next sc, sc in last sc; join with slip st to first sc: 168 sc.

Rnd 20: Ch 1, sc in same st and in next 5 sc, 2 sc in next sc, sc in next 14 sc, 2 sc in next sc, sc in next 38 sc, 2 sc in next sc, (sc in next 14 sc, 2 sc in next sc) 3 times, sc in next 38 sc, 2 sc in next sc, sc in next 14 sc, 2 sc in next sc, sc in last 8 sc; join with slip st to first sc: 176 sc.

Rnd 21: Ch 1, sc in same st and in next 14 sc, 2 sc in next sc, sc in next 55 sc, 2 sc in next sc, (sc in next 15 sc, 2 sc in next sc) twice, sc in next 55 sc, 2 sc in next sc, sc in next 15 sc, 2 sc in last sc; join with slip st to first sc: 182 sc.

Rnd 22: Ch 1, sc in same st and in each sc around; join with slip st to first sc, finish off.

CROCHET RUG INSTRUCTIONS (continued)

PLANNED OVAL RUG

FINISHED SIZE: 25" x 40"
(63.5 cm x 101.5 cm)

Recycled Items: denim and/or chambray clothing

You will also need a crochet hook, size K (6.5 mm)

Our rug was made in the following color sequence (rounds): Red (5), Lt Blue (4), Blue (2), Med Blue (8), Red (2), Blue (2), and Med Blue (5)

Read Crochet Basics, page 154, before beginning project.

Prepare fabric and cut into ½" strips (12 mm).

Ch 30 loosely.

Rnd 1 (Right side): Sc in second ch from hook and in each ch across to last ch, 3 sc in last ch; working in free loops of beginning ch (Fig. 1, page 154), sc in next 27 chs, 2 sc in next ch; join with slip st to first sc: 60 sc.

Rnd 2: Ch 1, 2 sc in same st, sc in next 27 sc, 2 sc in each of next 3 sc, sc in next 27 sc, 2 sc in each of last 2 sc; join with slip st to first sc: 66 sc.

Rnd 3: Ch 1, sc in same st, 2 sc in next sc, sc in next 28 sc, 2 sc in next sc, (sc in next sc, 2 sc in next sc) twice, sc in next 28 sc, 2 sc in next sc, sc in next sc, 2 sc in next sc; join with slip st to first sc: 72 sc.

Rnd 4: Ch 1, 2 sc in same st, sc in next sc, 2 sc in next sc, sc in next 29 sc, 2 sc in next sc, (sc in next sc, 2 sc in next sc) 3 times, sc in next 29 sc, (2 sc in next sc, sc in next sc) twice; join with slip st to first sc: 80 sc.

Rnd 5: Ch 1, sc in same st and in next sc, 2 sc in next sc, sc in next 33 sc, 2 sc in next sc, (sc in next 2 sc, 2 sc in next sc) twice, sc in next 33 sc, 2 sc in next sc, sc in next 2 sc, 2 sc in last sc; join with slip st to first sc: 86 sc.

Rnd 6: Ch 1, 2 sc in same st, sc in next 2 sc, 2 sc in next sc, sc in next 33 sc, 2 sc in next sc, (sc in next 2 sc, 2 sc in next sc) 3 times, sc in next 33 sc, (2 sc in next sc, sc in next 2 sc) twice; join with slip st to first sc: 94 sc.

Rnd 7: Ch 1, sc in same st and in next 2 sc, 2 sc in next sc, sc in next 36 sc, 2 sc in next sc, (sc in next 4 sc, 2 sc in next sc) twice, sc in next 36 sc, 2 sc in next sc, sc in next 4 sc, 2 sc in next sc, sc in last sc; join with slip st to first sc: 100 sc.

Rnd 8: Ch 1, sc in same st, 2 sc in next sc, sc in next 4 sc, 2 sc in next sc, sc in next 34 sc, 2 sc in next sc, (sc in next 4 sc, 2 sc in next sc) 3 times, sc in next 34 sc, 2 sc in next sc, sc in next 4 sc, 2 sc in next sc, sc in last 3 sc; join with slip st to first sc: 108 sc.

Rnd 9: Ch 1, sc in same st and in next 4 sc, 2 sc in next sc, sc in next 41 sc, 2 sc in next sc, (sc in next 5 sc, 2 sc in next sc) twice, sc in next 41 sc, 2 sc in next sc, sc in next 5 sc, 2 sc in last sc; join with slip st to first sc: 114 sc.

Rnd 10: Ch 1, sc in same st and in next sc, 2 sc in next sc, sc in next 6 sc, 2 sc in next sc, sc in next 35 sc, 2 sc in next sc, (sc in next 6 sc, 2 sc in next sc) 3 times, sc in next 35 sc, 2 sc in next sc, sc in next 6 sc, 2 sc in next sc, sc in last 4 sc; join with slip st to first sc: 122 sc.

Rnd 11: Ch 1, sc in same st and in next 5 sc, 2 sc in next sc, sc in next 46 sc, 2 sc in next sc, (sc in next 6 sc, 2 sc in next sc) twice, sc in next 46 sc, 2 sc in next sc, sc in next 6 sc, 2 sc in last sc; join with slip st to first sc: 128 sc.

Rnd 12: Ch 1, sc in same st and in next sc, 2 sc in next sc, sc in next 7 sc, 2 sc in next sc, sc in next 39 sc, 2 sc in next sc, (sc in next 7 sc, 2 sc in next sc) 3 times, sc in next 39 sc, 2 sc in next sc, sc in next 7 sc, 2 sc in next sc, sc in last 5 sc; join with slip st to first sc: 136 sc.

Rnd 13: Ch 1, sc in same st and in next 6 sc, 2 sc in next sc, sc in next 51 sc, 2 sc in next sc, (sc in next 7 sc, 2 sc in next sc) twice, sc in next 51 sc, 2 sc in next sc, sc in next 7 sc, 2 sc in last sc; join with slip st to first sc: 142 sc.

Rnd 14: Ch 1, sc in same st and in next sc, 2 sc in next sc, sc in next 8 sc, 2 sc in next sc, sc in next 43 sc, 2 sc in next sc, (sc in next 8 sc, 2 sc in next sc) 3 times, sc in next 43 sc, 2 sc in next sc, sc in next 8 sc, 2 sc in next sc, sc in last 6 sc; join with slip st to first sc: 150 sc.

Rnd 15: Ch 1, sc in same st and in next 8 sc, 2 sc in next sc, sc in next 54 sc, 2 sc in next sc, (sc in next 9 sc, 2 sc in next sc) twice, sc in next 54 sc, 2 sc in next sc, sc in next 9 sc, 2 sc in last sc; join with slip st to first sc: 156 sc.

Rnd 16: Ch 1, sc in same st and in next 4 sc, 2 sc in next sc, sc in next 10 sc, 2 sc in next sc, sc in next 44 sc, 2 sc in next sc, (sc in next 10 sc, 2 sc in next sc) 3 times, sc in next 44 sc, 2 sc in next sc, sc in next 10 sc, 2 sc in next sc, sc in last 5 sc; join with slip st to first sc: 164 sc.

Rnd 17: Ch 1, sc in same st and in next 9 sc, 2 sc in next sc, sc in next 57 sc, 2 sc in next sc, (sc in next 11 sc, 2 sc in next sc) twice, sc in next 57 sc, 2 sc in next sc, sc in next 11 sc, 2 sc in next sc, sc in last sc; join with slip st to first sc: 170 sc.

Rnd 18: Ch 1, sc in same st and in next 4 sc, 2 sc in next sc, sc in next 12 sc, 2 sc in next sc, sc in next 45 sc, 2 sc in next sc, (sc in next 12 sc, 2 sc in next sc) 3 times, sc in next 45 sc, 2 sc in next sc, sc in next 12 sc, 2 sc in next sc, sc in last 7 sc; join with slip st to first sc: 178 sc.

Rnd 19: Ch 1, sc in same st and in next 11 sc, 2 sc in next sc, sc in next 60 sc, 2 sc in next sc, (sc in next 13 sc, 2 sc in next sc) twice, sc in next 60 sc, 2 sc in next sc, sc in next 13 sc, 2 sc in next sc, sc in last sc; join with slip st to first sc: 184 sc.

Rnd 20: Ch 1, sc in same st and in next 5 sc, 2 sc in next sc, sc in next 14 sc, 2 sc in next sc, sc in next 46 sc, 2 sc in next sc, (sc in next 14 sc, 2 sc in next sc) 3 times, sc in next 46 sc, 2 sc in next sc, sc in next 14 sc, 2 sc in next sc, sc in last 8 sc; join with slip st to first sc: 192 sc.

Rnd 21: Ch 1, sc in same st and in next 14 sc, 2 sc in next sc, sc in next 63 sc, 2 sc in next sc, (sc in next 15 sc, 2 sc in next sc) twice, sc in next 63 sc, 2 sc in next sc, sc in next 15 sc, 2 sc in last sc; join with slip st to first sc: 198 sc.

Rnd 22: Ch 1, sc in same st and in next 7 sc, 2 sc in next sc, sc in next 16 sc, 2 sc in next sc, sc in next 47 sc, 2 sc in next sc, (sc in next 16 sc, 2 sc in next sc) 3 times, sc in next 47 sc, 2 sc in next sc, sc in next 16 sc, 2 sc in next sc, sc in last 8 sc; join with slip st to first sc: 206 sc.

Rnd 23: Ch 1, sc in same st and in next 16 sc, 2 sc in next sc, sc in next 66 sc, 2 sc in next sc, (sc in next 17 sc, 2 sc in next sc) twice, sc in next 66 sc, 2 sc in next sc, sc in next 17 sc, 2 sc in last sc; join with slip st to first sc: 212 sc.

Rnd 24: Ch 1, sc in same st and in next 7 sc, 2 sc in next sc, sc in next 18 sc, 2 sc in next sc, sc in next 48 sc, 2 sc in next sc, (sc in next 18 sc, 2 sc in next sc) 3 times, sc in next 48 sc, 2 sc in next sc, sc in next 18 sc, 2 sc in next sc, sc in last 10 sc; join with slip st to first sc: 220 sc.

Rnd 25: Ch 1, sc in same st and in next 18 sc, 2 sc in next sc, sc in next 69 sc, 2 sc in next sc, (sc in next 19 sc, 2 sc in next sc) twice, sc in next 69 sc, 2 sc in next sc, sc in next 19 sc, 2 sc in last sc; join with slip st to first sc: 226 sc.

Rnd 26: Ch 1, sc in same st and in next 9 sc, 2 sc in next sc, sc in next 20 sc, 2 sc in next sc, sc in next 49 sc, 2 sc in next sc, (sc in next 20 sc, 2 sc in next sc) 3 times, sc in next 49 sc, 2 sc in next sc, sc in next 20 sc, 2 sc in next sc, sc in last 10 sc; join with slip st to first sc: 234 sc.

Rnd 27: Ch 1, sc in same st and in next 19 sc, 2 sc in next sc, sc in next 74 sc, 2 sc in next sc, (sc in next 20 sc, 2 sc in next sc) twice, sc in next 74 sc, 2 sc in next sc, sc in next 20 sc, 2 sc in last sc; join with slip st to first sc: 240 sc.

Rnd 28: Ch 1, sc in same st and in each sc around; join with slip st to first sc, finish off.

INDEX

A-B

Aluminum Angel Plant Pokes, 57
Aluminum Can Flower Plant Pokes, 55
Aluminum Can Jewelry, 61
Aluminum Can Pins, 100
Aluminum Can Tree, 103
Appliquéd Coverlet Vest, 44
Belt Napkin Rings with Napkins, 92
Book Cover Frame, 68
Bottle Cap Doll, 118
Brown Paper Frame, 28
Button Mosaic Table, 95

C

Can Embellished Frames, 89
Can Luminary with Jar Votive, 11
CANDLES & CANDLEHOLDERS:
    Can Luminary with Jar Votive, 11
    Coffee Can Luminary, 75
    Drinking Glass Candleholder Jar, 125
    Floating Flower Candles, 54
    Game Piece-Covered Candles, 94
Candy Box Valentine Container, 99
Cap-Studded Serving Crate, 88
Cardboard Bill Organizer, 65
Cardboard Castle Centerpiece, 117
Cardboard Fishing Pole, 30
Cardboard Stands for Frames, 32
CD Christmas Ornament, 122
Chenille and Sock Scraps Lamb, 39
CHILDREN'S TOYS & ACCESSORIES:
    Candy Box Valentine Container, 99
    Cardboard Castle Centerpiece, 117
    Chenille and Sock Scraps Lamb, 39
    Ottoman Learning Center, 83
    Plastic Lid Faces Mobile, 79
    Tablecloth Butterfly Costume, 111

D

Découpaged Plastic Basket, 101
Denim Bolster Pillow, 38
Denim-Covered Containers, 69
Denim-Covered Wall Letters, 18
Drinking Glass Candleholder Jar, 125

CHRISTMAS TREE TRIMS:
    CD Christmas Ornament, 122
    Lid Snowman Tree Topper, 124
    Lightbulb Ornaments, 127
    Milk Carton Ornament, 123
CLOCKS:
    Mosaic-Tiled Saucer Clock, 58
    Wristwatch Wall Clock, 21
CLOTHING & JEWELRY:
    Aluminum Can Jewelry, 61
    Aluminum Can Pins, 100
    Appliquéd Coverlet Vest, 44
    Matchbox Pendant, 62
    Vintage Fabric-Embellished Shirt, 43
Coffee Can Lampshade, 10
Coffee Can Luminary, 75
Coffee Can Table and Soda-Can Vine, 27
CONTAINERS & ORGANIZERS:
    Candy Box Valentine Container, 99
    Cap-Studded Serving Crate, 88
    Cardboard Bill Organizer, 65
    Covered Boxes, 25
    Découpaged Plastic Basket, 101
    Denim-Covered Containers, 69
    Egg-Carton Trinket Keeper, 63
    Fleece-Covered Can Snowmen, 121
    Hanging Storage Bag, 48
    Leather Paperweights, 45
    Mailing Center, 17
    Matchbox Desk Organizer, 15
    Pin Cushion-Topped Can Notions Holder, 49
    Placemat Needlework Organizer, 47
    Soda-Can Palm Tree and Pencil Hut, 13
    Studded Cigar Box, 59
Covered Boxes, 25
Craft Scraps Collage, 77
Crocheted Rugs, 51
Cut-Out Gift Box, 115

E-F

Egg-Carton Trinket Keeper, 63
Faux-Finished Brass Floor Lamp and Lampshade Cover, 91
Fleece-Covered Can Snowmen, 121
Floating Flower Candles, 54
Framed Bed Tray, 87
Framed Quilt-Block Paper Art, 71
FRAMES/PHOTO DISPLAYS:
    Book Cover Frame, 68
    Brown Paper Frame, 28
    Can Embellished Frames, 89
    Cardboard Stands for Frames, 32
    Recycled Frames, 31
FURNITURE & HOME ACCESSORIES:
    Button Mosaic Table, 95
    Coffee Can Table and Soda-Can Vine, 27
    Crocheted Rugs, 51
    Framed Bed Tray, 87
    Painted Stool, 85
    Stamped Florals, 23

G-H

Game Piece-Covered Candles, 94
GIFT WRAP:
    Cut-Out Gift Box, 115
    Marbleized Paper for Gift Wrap and Tags, 112
    Recycled Cards Gift Boxes, 114
Halloween Jar Lamp, 107
Hanging Storage Bag, 48
HOLIDAY CRAFTS:
    Aluminum Can Pins, 100
    Aluminum Can Tree, 103
    Candy Box Valentine Container, 99
    CD Christmas Ornament, 122
    Découpaged Plastic Basket, 101
    Drinking Glass Candleholder Jar, 125
    Fleece-Covered Can Snowmen, 121
    Halloween Jar Lamp, 107
    Lid Snowman Tree Topper, 124
    Lightbulb Ornaments, 127
    Milk Carton Ornament, 123
    Natural Topiary Tree, 119
    Painted Vinyl Wall Hanging, 104
    Plastic Foam Wreath, 105
    Plastic Spider, 108

HOME DÉCOR:
- Aluminum Can Tree, 103
- Natural Topiary Tree, 119
- Paper Shelf Sitter, 76
- Plastic Foam Wreath, 105
- Textured Plastic Balls, 93

K-L

KITCHEN ACCESSORIES:
- Belt Napkin Rings with Napkins, 92
- Cap-Studded Serving Crate, 88
- Plastic Message Boards and Marker Holder, 70
- Table Leg Towel Holder, 84

LAMPS & LAMPSHADES:
- Coffee Can Lampshade, 10
- Faux-Finished Brass Floor Lamp and Lampshade Cover, 91
- Halloween Jar Lamp, 107
- Leather Paperweights, 45
- Lid Snowman Tree Topper, 124
- Lightbulb Ornaments, 127

M-N

- Mailing Center, 17
- Marbleized Paper for Gift Wrap and Tags, 112
- Matchbox Desk Organizer, 15
- Matchbox Pendant, 62
- Milk Carton Ornament, 123
- Mosaic-Tiled Saucer Clock, 58
- Natural Topiary Tree, 119

O

- Ottoman Learning Center, 83

OUTDOOR DÉCOR:
- Aluminum Angel Plant Pokes, 57
- Aluminum Can Flower Plant Pokes, 55
- Coffee Can Luminary, 75
- Mosaic-Tiled Saucer Clock, 58
- Outdoor Jewelry Decoration, 29
- Plastic Bottle Birdhouses, 73
- Plastic Spider, 108
- Outdoor Jewelry Decoration, 29

P

- Painted Bottle Vases, 19
- Painted Stool, 85
- Painted Vinyl Wall Hanging, 104
- Paper Shelf Sitter, 76
- Paper-Covered Boxes, 113

PARTY FAVORS/CENTERPIECES:
- Bottle Cap Doll, 118
- Cardboard Castle Centerpiece, 117
- Paper-Covered Boxes, 113
- Patriotic Paper Collage, 9

PILLOWS:
- Denim Bolster Pillow, 38
- Tablecloth Pillows, 41
- Pin Cushion-Topped Can Notions Holder, 49
- Placemat Needlework Organizer, 47
- Plastic Bottle Birdhouses, 73
- Plastic Foam Wreath, 105
- Plastic Lid Faces Mobile, 79
- Plastic Message Boards and Marker Holder, 70
- Plastic Spider, 108

R-T

- Recycled Cards Gift Boxes, 114
- Recycled Frames, 31
- Shredded Paper Vase, 67
- Soda-Can Palm Tree and Pencil Hut, 13
- Soda-Can Trout, 33
- Stamped Florals, 23
- Stringer of Fish, 33
- Studded Cigar Box, 59
- Table Leg Towel Holder, 84
- Tablecloth Butterfly Costume, 111
- Tablecloth Eye Soother, 37
- Tablecloth Pillows, 41
- Textured Plastic Balls, 93

V-W

VASES:
- Painted Bottle Vases, 19
- Shredded Paper Vase, 67
- Vintage Fabric-Embellished Shirt, 43

WALL DÉCOR:
- Cardboard Fishing Pole, 30
- Craft Scraps Collage, 77
- Denim-Covered Wall Letters, 18
- Framed Quilt-Block Paper Art, 71
- Painted Vinyl Wall Hanging, 104
- Patriotic Paper Collage, 9
- Soda-Can Trout, 33
- Stringer of Fish, 33
- Wristwatch Wall Clock, 21
- Wristwatch Wall Clock, 21

CREDITS

We want to extend a warm *thank you* to the generous people who allowed us to photograph our projects at their homes: Joan Adams, Diane Easley, Donna Harkins, Shirley Held, Ron and Catherine Hughes, Patti Kymer, Vicki Moody, Ellison Poe, Catherine Smith, Peggy Wilhelm, and Cheryl Wilson.

A special thanks goes to Viking Husqvarna Sewing Machine Company of Cleveland, Ohio, for providing the sewing machines used to create several of our projects. We also extend our gratitude to the following companies for providing us with their fine products: Design Master Color Tool of Boulder, Colorado; Walnut Hollow Farm of Dodgeville, Wisconsin; and Beacon Chemical Company of Mount Vernon, New York.

To photographers Jerry R. Davis of Jerry Davis Photography, Ken West of Peerless Photography, and Andrew Uilkie of Andrew Paul Photography, all of Little Rock, Arkansas, we say thank you for your time, patience, and excellent work.